The Silver Screens of Wirral

(A history of cinemas in Wallasey, Hoylake, West Kirby and South Wirral)

by

P.A. Carson and C.R. Garner

First published 1990 by Countyvise Limited, 1 & 3 Grove Road, Rock Ferry, Birkenhead, Wirral, Merseyside L42 3XS, and Metropolitan Borough of Wirral, Central Library, Borough Road, Birkenhead, Wirral L41 2XB.

ISBN No. 0 907768 36 9. Countyvise Limited.
ISBN No. 0 904582 10 8. Metropolitan Borough of Wirral.

Acknowledgement

The authors are indebted to many people who kindly donated information or photographs for use in this book. Whilst somewhat invidious to single out individuals they wish to record their thanks to the following. Mrs. B. Anderson (Wallasey), Mr. C. Bell (now living in Chirk), Mr. B. Bird (Wallasey), Mr. C. Bolton (Wallasey), Mr. I. Boumphrey (Prenton), Mr. F. Broadbent (Wallasey), Mr. G. Bryant (Eastham), Mr. A. Clayton (Wallasey), Mr. P. Dougherty (Port Sunlight), Mr. A. Eyles (London), Mr. R. Foster (Little Sutton), Mr. G. Houghton (Ellesmere Port), Mr. W. Houghton (Wallasey), Mrs. C. Gillespie (Liverpool), Mr. F. Gordon (Bromborough), Mrs. J. Hockey (Wallasey), Mr. N. Jenkins (Wallasey), Mr. T. Johnson (Neston), Mr. G. W. Kirkham (Ellesmere Port), Mr. F. Lindstrom (Irby), Mr. H. McQueen (Wallasey), Mr. D. Mitchelson (Bebington), Mr. C. Morris (Hoylake), Mr. G. Parker (Rock Ferry), Mr. S. Rebecca (Wallasey), Mr. W. Saxton (Liverpool) and Mr. D. Young (Pensby). Apologies are given to those who, quite unintentionally, escape due mention.

Gratitude is also extended to the North West Film Archive (Manchester Polytechnic) who provided two prints and to Mr. G. Weedon of the Fairground Heritage Trust. The authors were also impressed with the courteous and constructive service of the staff at the Public Libraries in Birkenhead, Ellesmere Port and Wallasey which facilitated the collection of relevant information and photographic material and generally removed much of the tedium from the research. Warm thanks also go to the staff of Wallasey Town Planning Dept. and to the management of The Top Rank Social Club and of the EPIC, both in Ellesmere Port.

Finally, the authors thank their families without whose support the text would not have been completed. In particular P.A.C. thanks his Wife, Kathleen, and their two sons, Paul and Neil, for their invaluable assistance with much of the laborious research of local papers. Kathleen also prepared the first typescript.

Dedication

The book is dedicated to:—

—a younger generation who wonder about the silver screens of a by-gone age.

—those who remember the silver screens yet still wonder.

—our wives, who wonder about us.

PAC/CRG

Preface

For some, the silver screens of yesteryear are simply remembered with nostalgia: the uniformed staff, the sparkling chandeliers, glittering fountains and sweeping marble staircases provided for ordinary people a form of escapism from the humdrum routine of the real world to the fantasy life-style of the stars on screen. For local historians, however, it is a record both of how the region adapted to, and applied, the emerging technology of electricity, cinematography, sound recording and amplification etc to mass entertainment, and how it exploited the new architectural opportunities for example in creating a combination of comfort and illusions of grandeur. As such this knowledge represents a valuable contribution to the social history of the region and adds to our appreciation of the life-style of the times. Furthermore, if one considers life on the peninsula to be a microcosm of that in Britain in general, then the fortunes of the cinema business in Wirral represent not only an important chapter in our local history but undoubtedly they provide an insight into the cinema industry throughout Britain. This relationship is confirmed by comparing UK cinema attendances between 1900 and the present day, with the pattern of the cinema business in Wirral over the same time span. Thus the Figure alongside shows that the distribution pattern of cinemas in Wirral parallels the figures for annual attendances at cinemas nation-wide.

When it was eventually realised that the era of picture houses as they were known had passed for ever, some cinema buffs recaptured the magic of the period by building their own picture palaces such as the eleven-seater cinema built by one of the present authors on to his semi-detached house in Wallasey, and the twenty-six seat Whitegates precast cinema built by Keith and Jean Maxwell in Carr Lane. The former boasts a five foot screen equipped with silver satin curtain and a rainbow of lights. Mr. Garner has a wide collection of vintage "shorts" and full-length dramas backed up by filmed organ music and over 30,000 old "78" records. The Whitegates is a purpose-built cinema fitted out with plush wall-to-wall carpets, a shimmering screen, dimmer wall-lights and a cloakroom and toilets. Mr. Maxwell is currently projectionist in Ellesmere Port at the EPIC.

The aim of this book, however, is to provide a glimpse at the region's commercial silver screens of bygone days. These distinctive buildings of the 1920's and 1930's represent an important contribution to our heritage of 20th century architecture, in much the same way as did the railway stations of the 19th century. The main source of information was local newspapers augmented by personal memories of the authors and those of a host of colleagues. Whilst extensive records are available for many cinemas there is a dearth of data available for some of the older picture-houses since they tended to rely more on advertisements displayed in the local shops than in the press.

For convenience this book is published in two volumes. The other book is dedicated to the cinemas of Bebington, Birkenhead, Claughton, New Ferry, Prenton, Rock Ferry and Tranmere. This book describes cinemas of the Wallasey region (Egremont, Liscard, Moreton, New Brighton, Seacombe and Wallasey) and the rest of the peninsular (Ellesmere Port, Heswall, Hoylake, Neston and West Kirby). Each volume contains a general introduction, which is common to both, tables summarising seating capacity, opening and closing dates for the cinemas in chronological order, plus maps identifying their location. The cinemas are arranged throughout in alphabetical order.

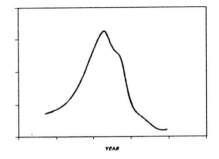

Trends in cinemas in Wirral

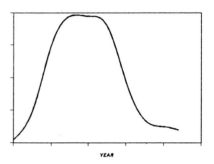

Attendances at UK cinemas

Introduction

The dawn of an era

The birth of films clearly has its roots in the development of photography but the true history of motion pictures is more accurately linked with the Kinetoscope. This device, invented by Thomas Edison in 1889, consisted of a peephole cabinet inside which an illuminated length of film revolved on spools to project the image on the end of the cabinet. Usually the machines were coin operated and the films were about fifty feet in length and ran for less than a minute. The subjects of Edison's films were simple such as a dog with a bone, a baby being bathed, a boxing match, and so on, all chosen to show movement, albeit rather jerky. The first public showing of *projected* moving pictures took place on the roof of Madison Square Garden on May 20th 1895 and later the same year Louis and Auguste Lumiere of Lyons presented their first projection machine at the first public film show in Paris in December 1895. It was on February 20th 1896 that the first public projected film show was given in Britain. This was at the Regent Street Polytechnic (Marlborough Hall), London.

It is astonishing that the film industry developed so rapidly as a form of viable entertainment from such humble beginnings, and the first films were shown on Merseyside as early as November 1896 at the Argyle, Birkenhead. Indeed, this was claimed to be the first film show outside London but records suggest that films may have been screened earlier in the year at the St. James Theatre and the old Y.M.C.A., both in Manchester. Following the early innovation at the end of the nineteenth century, the cinema industry on Wirral developed in four distinct phases.

The first stage was at the turn of the century when 'animated picture shows' and 'bioscopes' were to be seen at fairgrounds. These tended to be a simple tent set up behind a highly decorative facade built around two bioscope wagons, turning the bioscope into one of the largest and most ornate shows in the fair. A typical example is depicted in the illustration on the following page. Pioneers included Pat Collins who ran cinemas in Walsall, the potteries and in New Brighton. During this initial phase films were somewhat of a experiment. Thus the first moving pictures seen by Wallaseyans were those shown at Pat Collins' "The Big Show" in the Palace covered amusement park on the promenade, New Brighton. One of the early films to be shown at these twopenny side shows around 1903 was *The Mad Barber* which depicted a man having a shave: when the razor suddenly slipped his head rolled to the ground and then commenced to dance around the picture sheet. At that time the shows were changed once a month and were operated by the Excelsior Company in conjunction with variety featuring two small singers and dancers known as *Tiny and Mite*. Collins' funfair later travelled to other parts of the peninsula and, for example, gave a Christmas show at Birkenhead Market Place in 1909 which, in addition to rides, animal acts and side shows, included all the latest and best animated pictures.

In parallel with the Bioscope, films began to be shown in public halls and later progressed to become a regular feature of music hall programmes. It was during this second phase of development that the cinema became a more serious form of entertainment. It is reported that moving pictures were shown at the YMCA in Grange Road, Birkenhead in the late 1890's and in 1899 animated film shows were given by a Mr. Vanderbilt (real name Roberts) on the other side of the Wirral at the Public Hall, West Kirby. By 1900 performances of Saronie's (Vanderbilt's brother) Gold Medal Cinematograph were given at the Town Hall, Hoylake and the Tynwald Hall, West Kirby. However, it was not until 1911 when Messrs. G. Fenton and V. Branford began presenting films at West Kirby's Public Hall (later the Queens cinema) that the first regular picture shows arrived in this part of the Wirral. Later the following year these gentlemen extended their activities to Hoylake when they took lease on the Hoylake Institute (later the YMCA). The first time that animated pictures were advertised as the main attraction at a public hall in Wallasey was in September 1904 at the Irving Theatre.

During this period the new phenomenon was pre-occupied with establishing respectability and the 'halls' initially aligned themselves with the accepted theatre as a form of entertainment, and they often continued to be called 'theatres' even when their programmes consisted mainly of animated films. In the early 1900's some Wirral variety theatres such as The Argyle, The Theatre Royal and The Hippodrome all in Birkenhead and the Irving, The Palace and The Tower Theatres, all in the Wallasey area, included films in their bill of fare. After their novelty value had been exploited some music halls reverted to live variety. Even then, however, some retained News Reels at the end of their

A typical bioscope

programmes as "chasers" to encourage all but the true film-lovers to leave, thereby assisting to empty the halls. The Institute in Neston, the Church Institute at Ellesmere Port and the Kings Hall in Heswall were all similarly used as places of entertainment.

By this time the early films, in addition to providing light entertainment, soon covered more serious subjects such as the funeral of King Edward VI and the subsequent coronation of King George V and Queen Mary. Despite the general acceptance by now of moving pictures as an established type of entertainment the art form was not without its critics. Issues debated with the arrival of the motion pictures included the potential deleterious effect of films on morals and on health, particularly with respect to eyesight. (To some extent this apprehension of a new and emerging technology can be compared with modern-day concern expressed about a host of potential hazards associated with use of visual display units). Despite concern expressed about standards it is interesting to note that in 1928 alone the local Justices examined almost one-thousand film synopses yet banned only one film.

The next phase in the advancement of the industry was the conversion of existing buildings such as billiards halls and unused chapels into "electric palaces" as exemplified by the Globe in Birkenhead and the Lyceum Electric Palace in Egremont both in 1910, and the Wallasey Picturedrome and the Electric Picture Palace in Rock Ferry both in 1911. The growing popularity of the movies also resulted in the conversion of music halls into picture-houses as exemplified by the Queen's Hall in Birkenhead and Tranmere Music Hall, Old Chester Road.

The trend in the 1920's for the creation of purpose-built Picturedromes and Super Cinemas represents the fourth stage in the development of the picture-house. Here the tendency was to design in (or at least claim) the luxury which had been a feature of the interiors of earlier theatre buildings. Even their description as "picture palaces" and the choice of aristocratic or exotic name reflected an attempt to market the industry with a grandiose image. However, not all cinemas lived up to proprietors' claims and the smell of disinfectant, liberal use of scent sprays and colloquial reference to the premises by patrons as "flea pits" seemed in conflict with the market image. During the next two decades the facilities increased in luxury and sophistication with the arrival of such establishments as the Ritz, Regal, Plaza and the Gaumont (both in Birkenhead and Wallasey), with their neon lights, pile carpets, bucket seats and mighty Wurlitzer and Compton organs.

The 'Talkies' arrived on the Wirral first in Wallasey in June 1929 at The Royal in Egremont and in Birkenhead at The Scala in August the same year. This heralded a rapid growth of the industry with attendances rising dramatically in the late 1920's and early 1930's peaking at its heyday between 1930 and 1950 with about thirty cinemas operating on the Wirral. The arrival of the talkies however also presented problems for many in the industry as illustrated by the demise of cinema orchestras. Within a year of the talkies the operators and proprietors of some sixty cinemas on Merseyside were locked in conflict. The operators complained of long hours of work and the nervous strain associated with long-running talkie pictures. In September 1930 the operators and electricians voted for strike action and the proprietors retaliated with threats of using university students to man the projection equipment. All-out strikes were averted, however, when a compromise was reached and the operators settled for improved conditions and money.

Although most picture-goers in the early days tended to frequent local cinemas, they gradually became less parochial in their taste, a trend aided by the improvements in public transport (eg. expanded bus services, the electrification in 1938 of the Birkenhead to New Brighton line) and the increasing popularity of the private motor car.

For a brief spell at the onset of the Second World War picture houses had to close by government decree. This ruling was soon rescinded and most cinemas re-opened on the 18th September 1939. In many cases, box-office takings were down during the war years, although some pictures continued to be well attended with "House Full" signs on display as cinemas provided a valuable means of relief from the worries and hardship during these troubled years. This was particularly noticeable in the outlying regions of the peninsula as exemplified by the Tudor at West Kirby, where attendances were boosted by the influx of evacuees into the district from the bomb targets of Birkenhead and Wallasey. During the War, over 300 British cinemas were destroyed by enemy bombs. The Wirral did not escape the ravages of enemy action and those cinemas badly damaged or completely destroyed included the Avenue, Palladium, Plaza and Ritz in Birkenhead, the Winter Gardens in New Brighton and the Cosmo (Coliseum) in Wallasey. It was also during this period that Sunday opening of cinemas was introduced for parts of Wirral, but only after much controversy and resistance from the Church, councillors and Licensing judges. Thus in 1943 licences were granted to the three local cinemas in Ellesmere Port to show films between 5.30 and 9.30 pm, except those of H category. For some parts of the Wirral Sunday opening came much later eg. 1949 in Bebington and 1962 in Neston.

Between 1945 and 1954 the region was caught between the end of the War and an economic boom when people throughout the land flocked to the cinemas in their millions. This was the era of Crosby, Hope and Lamour in the *Road to...* films, Mickey Rooney in the *Andy Hardy* series, Westerns by John Ford such as *Stage Coach* and *Fort Apache* and the Gangster movies as exemplified by *Angels with Dirty Faces* and *The Roaring Twenties*.

The Cinemas That Never Were

It is of interest to note that during the period of expansion more cinemas were planned for the region than were actually built. Thus in 1937 an application by Messrs. Pain and Blease was approved for a £40,000 luxury cinema and dance hall at the northwesterly junction of Teehey Lane and Village Road, Higher Bebington. Plans showed the seating capacity to be around 1200, with 393 in the balcony and 800 in the stalls. The dance hall would hold a further 270. The cinema never left the drawing board.

Also in Birkenhead, plans were approved before the war for the erection of a cinema in Woodchurch Road which was to be called either the Curzon or the Rex. This would have been the last cinema designed by Sidney Colwyn Foulkes for SM Super Cinemas Ltd. According to the plans the lower section of the auditorium marked a return to the traditional type of design. The upper walls

IN TOWN TONIGHT

(1954)

ASTOR — Sabu, Raymond Massey in " The Drum" (U) plus " Seven Days to Noon" (A).

COLISEUM — John Payne, Evelyn Keyes in " 99 River Street" (A) 3.20, 6.48, 9.25, plus " Marshal's Daughter" (U) 2.5, 5.40, 8.19.

EMPIRE — John Garfield, Lilli Palmer in " Body and Soul" (A) 2.52, 5.45, 8.44, plus Donald Woods in " Undercover Agent" (U) 1.43, 4.39, 7.35.

GAUMONT — Yvonne de Carlo, Joel McCrea in " Border River" (U) 3.0, 6.10, 9.20, plus Frankie Howerd, Margaret Rutherford in " The Runaway Bus" (U) 1.20, 4.25, 7.35.

LYCEUM — Robert Taylor, Ava Gardner in " Ride Vaquero" (U) 3.45, 6.5, 9.20, plus Walter Pidgeon in " Unknown Man" (A) 2.5, 7.35.

PALACE — Joan Fontaine, Jack Palance in " Flight to Tangier" (U).

PLAZA — Richard Carlson, Barbara Rush in " It Came From Outer Space" (A) 3.10, 6.55, 9.5.

REGAL — Gregory Peck, Jane Griffiths in " The Million Pound Note" (U) 3.20, 6.20, 9.10, plus " Royal Symphony" (U) 2.0, 7.45.

RIALTO — Eileen Herlie, Cecil Parker in " Isn't Life Wonderful" (U) plus The Bowery Boys in " Loose in London" (U).

RIO — John Hodiak, Stephen McNally in " Battlezone" (A).

RITZ — Glenn Ford, Ann Sheridan in "Appointment in Honduras" (U) 3.10, 6.10, 9.10, plus Ronald Howard in " Flannelfoot" (A) 1.35, 4.35, 7.35.

ROXY — John Payne, Evelyn Keyes in " 99 River Street" (A) 3.41, 6.23, 9.5, plus Lauri Anders in " Marshall's Daughter" (U) 2.19, 5.1, 7.43.

SAVOY — Jack Hawkins, Elizabeth Allan in " Front Page Story" (A) 1.45, 5.20, 8.55, plus Alex Nichol, Eleanor Summerfield in " Face the Music" (A) 3.30, 7.5.

SUPER — Dean Martin, Jerry Lewis in " Money From Home" (U) 2.25, 5.40, 9.0, plus Tom Conway, Eva Bartok in " Park Plaza 605" (U) 1.0, 4.15, 7.35.

and ceiling were to be completely plain. The outline of the proscenium would have closely followed that of the screen at either side of which were to have been two slender columns. The lighting was to have been by the Holophane Co. In addition to auditorium and stage lighting effects, the white surround at the back of what would now be termed a "floating screen" was to have been lit during the showing of a film with colour lighting synchronised to add atmosphere and effect to the picture. By September 1939 the foundations of the cinema had been laid on land near to the Half Way House but the outbreak of war brought an abrupt halt to all cinema constructions. Sadly the picture house was never completed but it was not until the middle of 1956 that the land was eventually sold for alternative use.

Artist impression of Regal (Wallasey).

Plans were approved by the Wallasey Council's Works Committee on Wednesday 14th July 1937 for a new super cinema to be built on the site of the Central Market in Wallasey Road. The £40,000 - £50,000 Regal was designed by the architects, Messrs. M.W. and W.M. Shennan of Hamilton Square, Birkenhead. The plans were for a cinema with seating capacity for 2,108, a cafe, balcony and its own car park. However this project was not pursued.

Likewise, the 30,000 residents of Bromborough were promised their own cinema in April 1930. Details for a 880 seater picture house were presented to the planners on behalf of Mr. F.G.B. Scaddy of 'Heathstone', Spital Road, Bromborough. The cinema was to be erected 70 yards from Bromborough Cross in Allport Lane on a site occupied by 'The Hollies' dwelling house. It was to be built in the Georgian style from rustic bricks and artificial stone dressing. Two small shops were to flank the main entrance. Inside, a stage and dressing room facilities were planned to enable small plays to be presented. The application was supported by Mr. A. Earnest Shennan of Liverpool, who emphasised the modern features which were embodied in the proposals, including the isolated operating suite to which access was gained only via a separate exterior entrance. Despite objections by Superintendent Ennion the proposal was approved but in the event Bromborough's cinema was never built. At the time of writing this book, plans were muted to build an entertainment complex in Bromborough housing a multi-screen unit, and so the 'village' may yet have its own cinema, albeit 60 years late!

The Cinema Organs

The arrival of the talkies heralded the end for orchestral accompaniment to the films and provided impetus for the cinema organists to display their talents as they became an integral part of new larger establishments. It is worthy of note that Birkenhead can claim to be the spiritual home of cinema organs since it was a Birkenhead man, Hope Jones, who first introduced electric action into organs in his workshop in Argyle Street. The Rialto in New Ferry and the Plaza, Regal and Ritz in Birkenhead all had Comptons (although after bomb damage the instrument at the Ritz was replaced by a Christie organ which had been reconditioned by Wurlitzer). Interestingly, there were more cinemas with organs in the Birkenhead area than elsewhere on the peninsula which tends to reflect the differences in age of the cinemas in the various parts of the region. Indeed, had the Regal been built, which had been planned for Wallasey in 1937, this would have been the first picture house in that part of the Wirral which had a theatre organ. The organ from the Regal, Birkenhead, was eventually transferred to the Winter Gardens in New Brighton.

Cinema organists became local and national celebrities in their own right, exemplified by Rowland Tims, Sydney Gustard, Lewis Oddie and Frank Gordon who were household names. Thus, Mr. Lewis Oddie, a Yorkshire man born in Brockhole became the local church organist at the age of twelve and had his first experience as a cinema organist when he went to America just before the First World War. Mr. Oddie was recruited to play the new organ in the Plaza in Birkenhead. This 3 manual/12 rank Compton, at the time, was the largest on Merseyside. Mr. Oddie was a regular radio broadcaster and a popular figure at the Plaza where he remained as resident organist until his untimely death in 1936. As a mark of respect the staff, commissionaires, attendants, page boys etc., in their blue and gold uniforms lined up outside the cinema as a guard of honour as Mr. Oddie's funeral cortege passed by. Mr. Frank Gordon became equally renowned as a local organist and radio broadcaster. Mr. Gordon, a Mancunian by birth, like Mr. Oddie began as a young church organist at fourteen years of age. Three years later he became resident pianist at Lewis', Manchester, by day and a ballroom danceband leader by night. In 1938 he succeeded Sydney Gustard, who had taken over duties from Mr. Oddie, as resident organist at the Plaza where he stayed until 1951, a period of employment broken only by his service with the Royal Navy in World War Two. In 1951 he moved to the Ritz where he played for a further six years during which time he was a regular radio broadcaster. At present Mr. Gordon lives in Ambleside Close, Bromborough and teaches organ students at his studio in Craines in Liverpool and is president of the Merseyside Organ Society. He still broadcasts and records for the BBC.

Sydney Gustard

Mr. Frank Gordon at the Christie Pipe Organ (Ritz) taken during a BBC recording session.

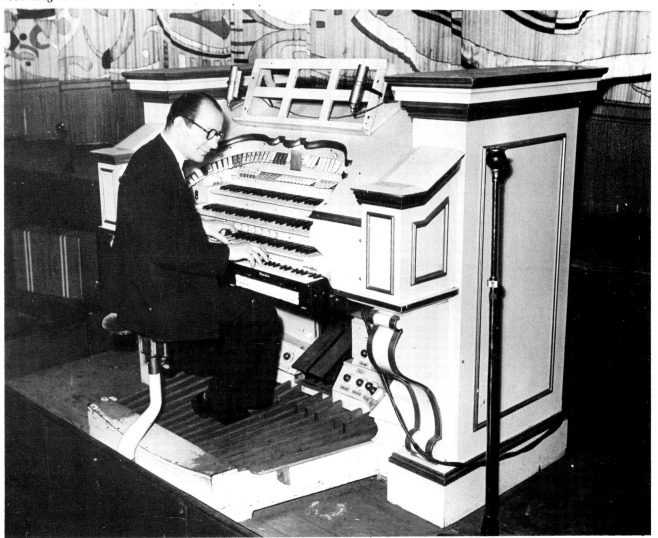

Henry Croudson and Lesley Walsh at the Regal (1939)

Mr. R. Saronie

The Impact of Cinema Owners and their Managers

Without a doubt the success of many picture-houses was directly attributable to the enterprise of their proprietors and management. As an illustration, James R. Saronie (real name Roberts), a Liverpool photographer and entrepeneur, began recording events of interest on film around Merseyside. His first films were just thirty feet long and took but a minute to screen. After some success with showing films at the YMCA and in halls across the peninsula, Mr. Saronie converted The Tranmere Music Hall, Old Chester Road, into the Coliseum (Picture Palace) in the first decade of the century. He went on to open the Electric Palace (later the Park Picture Hall) in Birkenhead and later the Scala at Prestatyn in North Wales where he made his home. The successful circuit, Bedford Cinemas Ltd., which owned many cinemas in the region at some stage of their life including the Lyceum (Egremont), Marina (New Brighton), Plaza (Birkenhead) and Trocadero (New Brighton), was created by Mr. J.F. Wood, who started in the early 1900's by renting the Queens Hall in Birkenhead and the Walton Baths Liverpool, for showing films. The venture proved so successful that by the end of that year he had built Liverpool's first purpose-built picture house, the Bedford Hall, Walton. Mr. Southan Morris started the SM chain whose aquisitions included the Kings (Heswall), Lyceum (New Ferry), Moreton Picture House, Neston New Cinema, Palladium and Picturedrome (both in Birkenhead), Queens (Ellesmere Port), Regal, Rio and Ritz (all in Birkenhead) and the Winter Gardens (both in Hoylake and in New Brighton).

The Gaumont - British Picture Corporation (formed in 1927 by Colonel A.C. Bromhead, Isidore Ostrer, C.M. Woolf, Michael Balcon and Lord Beaverbrook) owned the largest number of cinemas in Wirral, many of which formerly belonged to the Bedford chain.

Part I
Cinemas of Egremont, Liscard, Moreton, New Brighton, Seacombe and Wallasey

TABLE OF CINEMAS IN CHRONOLOGICAL ORDER OF OPENING

Date of Opening*	Date of Closing	Map Ref	Cinema	Seating Capacity	Architect
1885(1906)	1926	8	Palace/Gaiety Theatre	750	—
1885(1911)	1912	11	Wallasey Picturedrome	200	—
1897(1904)	1954	1	Tower Theatre	3000	—
1899(1904)	1959	15	Irving Theatre (later Kings/ Scala/Hippodrome/ Embassy.)	900	—
1907	1907	2	Hales Tours of the World	—	—
— (1907)	1914	16	Vienna Hall	—	—
1908	1931	9	Winter Gardens (previously Atherton Hall)	—	—
1862(1910)	1931	19	Lyceum Electric Palace	600	—
1911	1959	12	Liscard Electric Palace	700	—
1911	1959	17	Queens	800	—
— (1912)	1912	5	Picture Land	200	—
1912	1969	6	Court	450	—
— (1912)	1967	18	Royal	850	—
1913	1914	3	Daylight Cinema	c.300	—
1913	1941	10	Cosmo/Coliseum	700	—
— (1914)	1963	14	Old Court House/Kinema/ Kings/Continental	400	—
1914(1923)	1955	4	Tivoli	636	—
1916	1956	16	Marina	950	A. Shennan
1921	1964	20	Moreton Picture House	850	A. Shennan
1922	1956	7	Trocadero	900	Wright & Hamlyn
1926	1974	13	Capitol	1390	—
1931(1936)	1957	9	New Winter Gardens	1400	T. Taliesin
1933	present	19	Gaumont/Unit 4	1209	W.E. Trent
1951	1983	10	Phoenix	930	A Webber

* The date quoted refers to the opening of the building. The figure in brackets refers to the date films were first shown if this was different to the opening date.

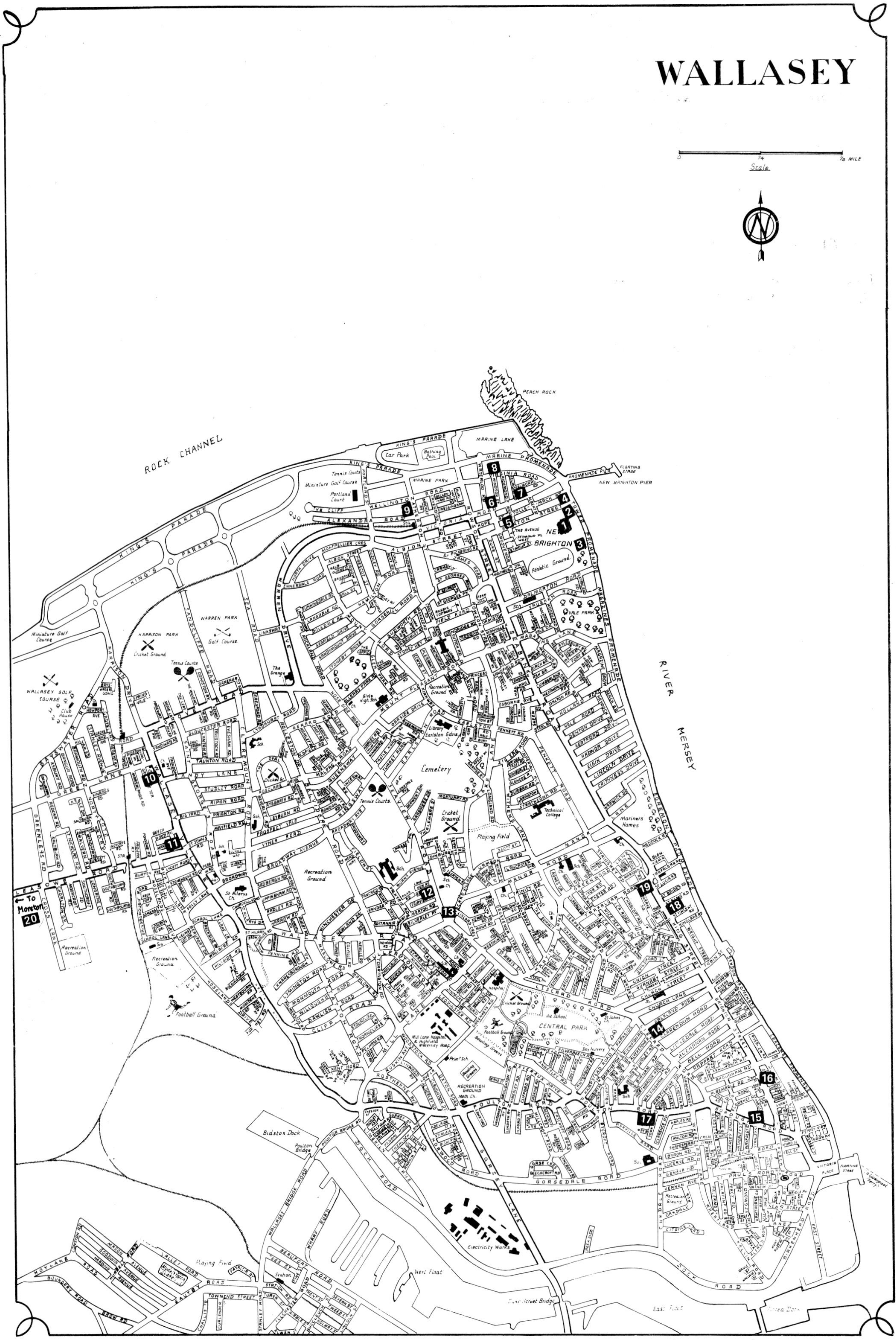

WALLASEY

Scale

N

PERCH ROCK

ROCK CHANNEL

KING'S PARADE

MARINE LAKE

Car Park

Bathing Pool

MARINE PROMENADE

PROMENADE PIER

FLOATING STAGE

NEW BRIGHTON PIER

Tennis Courts

Miniature Golf Course

Portland Courts

MARINE PARK

NE BRIGHTON

Athletic Ground

KING'S PARADE

ALEXANDRA ROAD

ALBION STREET

Miniature Golf Course

Vale Park

WARREN PARK

Golf Course

HARRISON PARK

Cricket Ground

Tennis Courts

The Grange

Recreation Ground

WALLASEY GOLF COURSE

Club House

RIVER MERSEY

Cemetery

Library

Tennis Courts

Cricket Ground

Technical College

Playing Field

Mariners Homes

TAUNTON ROAD

RIPON ROAD

Recreation Ground

St Albans

St Hilary

To Moreton

Recreation Ground

Recreation Ground

Football Ground

CENTRAL PARK

Hospital

Cricket Ground

Football Ground

Mill Lane Hospital & Highfield Maternity

Prim Sch

RECREATION GROUND

Bidston Dock

Poulton Bridge

GORSEDALE ROAD

Recreation Ground

VICTORIA PLACE

FLOATING STAGE

Electricity Works

Playing Field

Station

West Float

Duke Street Bridge

East Float

TOWNEND STREET

Capitol

What was to be Wallasey's most popular cinema opened in the centre of the shopping area in Liscard Village on Saturday the 4th September 1926 with *Midnight Sun* starring Laura La Plante and Pat O'Malley. The inauguration of this 1,390 seater picture-house was performed by the Mayor, Alderman J.W. Holdsworth and the proceeds from the opening performance (which amounted to £22.9.9) were donated to the Victoria Central Hospital. A full orchestra under the direction of a local musician provided musical entertainment.

The cinema was built by the owners, Messrs. Horricks Bros. of Wallasey, on a site previously occupied by a block of stable yards known as Gibbons Corner. The building comprised a cafe with provision for dancing, fifteen lock-up shops and office accommodation, in addition to the picture-house.

The imposing frontage of the building was finished in glazed terracotta with a large verandah to afford patrons queueing outside some protection from the elements. Adjacent to the foyer, with its central box office and a terrazzo floor, was a spacious waiting-room.

The auditorium was extremely lofty with four ornamental grilles in the ceiling which concealed air ducts equipped with high-powered electric fans to provide efficient ventilation. Six large Electroliers suspended from the ceiling provided the main auditorium illumination which was supplemented by glass flambeaux fittings on the lower side walls. The encircling walls themselves were lined at ground level with mahogany panels and were decorated above in shades of cream and brown. Seats were arranged on a stepped floor both in the stalls and the balcony to give added comfort for the feet. The proscenium, which was framed in intricate fibrous plaster work, was surmounted by a prominent feature depicting three galleons in full sail, and the whole set off by deep crimson velvet curtains edged in gold with matching pelmet. Both these, and the screen curtains, were hand controlled from within the projection room.

Capitol (1946)

Capitol (1957)

Capitol (1957)

Capitol (ABC) re-opening (9th November 1959)

The first manager was Percy Inkester and prices were 6d, 8d, 1/- and 1s 2d. Included in the Capitol building was a music shop run by Messrs. R.A. Strother, where cinema patrons could purchase records of any music played by the orchestra.

To celebrate Birthday week a year later in September 1927, 'Patrizov — The Wizard of the Violin' (formerly of the Futurist, Liverpool) took over leadership of the celebrated Capitol Orchestra, but on the 1st July 1929 the voice of Al Jolson in *The Singing Fool* brought the latest sensation of "talking pictures" to the Capitol, (just one week after the Royal introduced talkies to Wallasey). By August Patrizov and his orchestra had been relegated to the Capitol Cafe. Unfortunately the early talkie apparatus was not compatible with the lofty height and the poor acoustics of the Capitol auditorium. One measure taken to improve sound quality was a series of steel wires stretched at intervals across the auditorium at cornice level designed to deflect the sound downwards. However, it was not until the Capitol was taken over by Associated British Cinema in later years that the problem was properly resolved by the installation of new sound equipment first in May 1936 and, again in July 1940, when Western Electric Mirrorphonic Sound was fitted. For a brief spell in November 1934 there was a reversion to live music when Jerry Mack and his band and Ralph Wynn, the celebrated tap dancer, appeared on stage to supplement film programmes.

No further changes occurred at the Capitol until CinemaScope was installed in February 1955. In September 1959 the theatre then closed for two months to undergo a complete modernisation programme. The Capitol re-opened as Wallasey's new ABC Cinema on Monday the 9th November 1959 with a special gala performance of *Carry on Teacher* in the presence of the Mayor of Wallasey. Also present was Peter Kilby at the Hammond Electric Organ and the Fanfare Trumpeters of the Royal Corps. of Signals.

Outside the old glass verandah had disappeared and a modern internally-lit advertising screen installed. But it was inside that the real transformation had taken place. Modifications included removal of large sections of the old fibrous plasterwork from the walls and installation of a giant new screen which covered the original proscenium, with wall-to-wall curtaining illuminated by floods situated on the front of the circle. Also there were fewer, but more-capacious seats, and in the foyer the pay-box and stairs had been re-aligned. However, despite its striking new image, the ABC never seemed to recover its former popularity, and manager Bill Roberts claimed that during the period of closure many former patrons had found alternative forms of entertainment and had failed to return.

As with many of its contemporaries, the ABC suffered from the drop in popularity in cinemas. Towards the end of 1973 there were plans for the stalls area to be used for bingo with a cinema in the circle, but the local council stipulated that a lift would have to be provided for the benefit of the disabled, a condition that was obviously unacceptable to ABC who closed the theatre on the 23rd of February 1974 with a showing of Cliff Richard's *Take Me High* and Jack Palance in *The Big and the Bad.*

Several applications were put to the Council to convert the premises for alternative forms of entertainment such as bingo and these met with various forms of resistance. The first objection in 1977 was on the grounds that the site provided inadequate car parking facilities. Another application later the same year was rejected on a technicality: EMI rivals, Mecca, objected because the proposals notice had not been displayed outside the building for fourteen consecutive days. Since the local gaming committee met but once a year, this tactic resulted in a twelve month delay. Eventually, however, bingo did arrive in 1978.

20

Cosmo
(Coliseum)

Whit Monday, the 12th of May 1913, was the opening date for Wallasey's newest cinema, advertised as hygienic and comfortable with a superb programme of animated pictures, the first of which was *For the Honour of the 7th*, described as a stirring war drama. A further attraction was the "unrivalled Cosmo orchestra" under Ernest Rumbold, late leader in H.M. Grenadier Guards. Programmes were continuous from 3.00 to 10.30 p.m. at prices of 3d, 6d and 1/-.

Seating was provided for 700 on one floor and the decor in the auditorium was similar to that of the Queens. The frontage included four shops and was surmounted by a central glass dome with a spiral staircase behind leading to the projection room. An electric generator was housed in a shed behind one of the shops to supply direct current for the projector arcs, but theatre lighting was from the town supply. Entrance to the single storey auditorium was through an elegant red-carpeted octagonal foyer decorated with potted palms.

Throughout its twenty eight years in existence this theatre underwent several changes in ownership, management and entertainment policy. From the winter of 1917 onwards the cinema was advertised as The Cosy Cosmo, the lessee at this time being Frank Weston. By 1924, the Cosmo was under the control of F.V. Ross, already well known in Wallasey for his association with the Hippodrome and Tivoli Theatres. After the addition of a 40ft. deep stage with fly tower and nine dressing rooms, the Cosmo re-opened as the Coliseum Theatre on Monday the 24th June 1924. It was claimed that the theatre was one of the prettiest and most comfortable of its kind on Merseyside. The general decorative scheme was in Prussian blue, white and gold. The carpet and seat upholstery were in rich blue velvet pile and curtains of the same colour edged in gold. The ceiling was white and the walls finished in a yellow tone. The manager was G.W.E. Campion and the opening programme was Charles Wade's 'Concord' Company, described as a Super Concert Party. Prices were 9d, 1/3 and 1/10 with performances once nightly except on Saturdays when two performances were staged.

Cosmo during World War I

THE COSMO,
WALLASEY VILLAGE.

"Behold in us what leisure hour's demand,
Amusement and instruction, hand in hand."

GRAND OPENING WHIT WEEK,

THE LATEST AND MOST UP-TO-DATE PICTURE
HOUSE.
HYGIENIC AND COMFORTABLE.
A Superb Programme of Animated Pictures.
CONTINUOUS PERFORMANCE 3 p.m. to 10-30 p.m.

PRICES .. 5d., 6d., 1s.
CHILDREN 2d., 3d., 6d.

THE COSMO ORCHESTRA IS
UNRIVALLED.

THE COSMO,
WALLASEY VILLAGE.

"Behold in us what leisure hour's demand,
Amusement and instruction, hand in hand."

MONDAY, TUESDAY AND WEDNESDAY—
"FOR THE HONOUR OF THE 7TH,"
A STIRRING WAR DRAMA.

THURSDAY, FRIDAY AND SATURDAY—
"THE MAN WE MIGHT HAVE
BEEN."

Daily Continuous Performance 7 to 10·40 p.m.
Doors open 6·30 p.m.
Matinees, Mondays and Saturday at 3 p.m.
Doors open 2·30 p.m.
Prices—Circle 1s., Stalls 6d., Pit 6d.
Children ,, 6d. ,, 3d. ,, 2
THE FAMOUS COSMO ORCHESTRA
UNRIVALLED.

Wallasey's New Theatre.

OPENING OF THE COLISEUM.

Transformed from a picture house into
a cosy and luxuriously furnished theatre,
the Wallasey Coliseum, hitherto the Cosmo,
opened its doors on Monday evening. The
management claim that the theatre is one
of the prettiest and most comfortable of
its kind on Merseyside and certainly there
is much to support that claim. The general
decorative scheme is Prussian blue, white
and gold—a very successful and artistic
blending. The carpet and seat upholstery
are of rich blue velvet pile and the curtains
are the same colour velvet edged with gold.
The ceiling is white and the walls a yellow
tone. The stage is large, being forty feet
deep, and the lighting is especially good.

A GOOD OPENING.

The management could hardly have done
better than in securing Charles Wade's "Concord" Company for the opening week. This
company, which is of the super concert party
type, never fails to score a hit, for both
individual and concerted numbers are of
a high standard. Charles Wade possesses
a rich baritone voice and sings delightfully
several old favourites, while Bert Alden
proves himself a true humorist in both song
and dialogue. Syd. Glyn adds to the fun
with song and dance, the latter being particularly bright. As Mrs. 'Arris Miss Saxon
Davis is deservedly much appreciated, her
songs and dances being additional attractions.
Miss Nancy Sutcliffe has a charming voice
and knows how to use it, and Miss Arabella
Allen in some of her famous Dickens characters provides one of the best things of the
evening. Will Edwards, the accompanist,
does his part very ably and in a turn of his
own touches a high level. The show is
well rounded off with some clever concerted
numbers and sketches.

The programme was changed on Thursday.
To-night (Saturday) there will be two
performances at 6·45 and 8·45.

Cosmo (circa 1915)

It seems that stage entertainment was not a success, as from Easter Monday
1925 there was a reversion to films, with a change of management and the theatre
now re-named Wallasey Picture House. The first film programme shown by the
new management was 'The Family Secret' starring Baby Peggy and Gladys
Hulette, and the Apollo Orchestra was under the personal direction of Fred
Halliday. From September 1925, Mabel Stocks and her Wonderful Orchestra
were advertised, and by February 1927 there was a reversion to the name of
Coliseum, although pictures continued to be the main fare offered. At this time
500 tip-up seats were advertised at 8d and the manager was S.A. Jones. In
September 1929 a "Band Box Review" was advertised on stage together with the
full film programme, and from the 23rd December further stage-screen
programmes were advertised. The week of 20th January 1930 saw a brief
reversion to purely stage entertainment starting with a review called "All the
Best", featuring twelve beautiful scenes, admirably staged with the Desmond
Girls and Mlle. Veronica from the Winter Gardens in Berlin. Programmes were
twice nightly at 6.30 and 8.40 p.m.

On the 24th of March 1930, the Coliseum became Wallasey's latest Talking Theatre with an all-British talkie installation. The opening attraction was the all-talking, singing and dancing sensation, *Broadway Melody* featuring Bessie Love and Anita Page. In February 1931 the Coliseum was yet again under new management with the latest B.T.H. Talkie installation, new projectors and a new screen. The next year a scheme was announced for "important re-construction" by one of the big syndicates to provide a capacity of 1,500 with a balcony holding 350, but nothing further was to be heard of these plans.

Saturday afternoon children's matinees with all seats costing 2d were to become a popular feature at the Coliseum during the 1930's and there were no further changes till the war came. In common with all places of entertainment, the Coliseum closed on its outbreak and re-opened again two weeks later, and in January 1940 Sunday concerts organised by a Mr. C.W. Binks were being staged. However, German air raids later in 1940 caused cinemas to curtail their evening performances which now started an hour earlier in order to finish at 9.30 p.m. Of course, these air raids also caused a drastic drop in cinema attendances which finally led to the closure of the theatre on Saturday the 9th November with the film *Middle Watch* starring Jack Buchanan. This was announced as a temporary closure, but in March 1941 a direct hit by a German bomb caused extensive damage that led to the demolition of the Coliseum soon afterwards.

Coliseum after bomb damage
(1941)

COLISEUM VILLAGE, WALLASEY

Matinees Monday, Wednesday and Saturday, at 3 p.m. Prices 6d. and 9d.
Evenings 6-40 to 10-40. Continuous. Prices 6d., 9d. and 1/3.
MONDAY, MARCH 24th, 1930—All Talking, Singing and Dancing Sensation—
"THE BROADWAY MELODY."
Featuring **BESSIE LOVE and ANITA PAGE.**
THURSDAY, MARCH 27th—THE 100% TALKING DRAMA—
"THREE BROTHERS."
Featuring **MATT MOORE, TOM MOORE, OWEN MOORE.**
SEE AND HEAR YOUR TALKIES ON THE NEW ALL BRITISH TALKING
APPARATUS. CLEAR TONE. PERFECT REPRODUCTION.

Court Cinema

The Court Cinema at 96/98 Victoria Road, owned by Mersey Halls Ltd., opened on the 16th December 1912. This was New Brighton's first purpose-built cinema and by most standards was a small, somewhat intimate theatre, attractively appointed and fitted-out with the best cinematic equipment, and adequate ventilation to keep the air fresh and cool without creating draught. It was described as "New Brighton's Cosy Picture Boudoir". The main thrust of the internal decor was of red and white with carpets, upholstery and light fittings setting the tone. Unfortunately little detail of the architecture was recorded in the local papers of the time. The officiation was performed by Mr. W. Ward-Platt, a local dignitary, with the manager, Mr. Douglas Stuart, in attendance. The platform was tastefully decorated for the occasion with palms and chrysanthemums. The opening films, which included *The Little Bear, Hydrogen, Henry VIII*, and *Romance at the Coast* were shown after a "bevy of grey-clad young ladies" served afternoon tea with chocolates for the children. Performances were continuous from 7.00 p.m. with matinees on Mondays, Wednesday and Saturdays with admission at 3d, 6d and 1/-. One patron of the Court in those early years remembers a smartly uniformed doorman handing out brightly coloured blotters, on the reverse side of which were printed details of the following week's programmes.

The next time the Court made news was on Monday the 13th August 1931, when "Perfect Talkies" were advertised, commencing with *Near Rainbow's End*, starring Bob Steele and Louise Lorraine, and *Borrowed Wives* with Rex Lease and Nita Norton. During the following two decades or so the Court survived several changes in management, and in August 1940 when Mr. W.J. Speakman took control, much-needed new talkie apparatus was installed and some refurbishment took place. After a period of closure in 1943 the Court re-opened in December of that year specialising as a News Theatre under the management of Charles Massey, formerly manager at the nearby Winter Gardens. This venture was short lived and normal programmes of feature films were re-instated two weeks later.

Major modifications, both internally and externally, were made after World War II when the theatre was bought by Whilma Wilkie, proprietor of the New Palace Amusement Park. Between the 29th of November and the 4th of December 1947 new Kalee projectors were on exhibition to the public in a nearby shop, specially rented for the purpose. This equipment was in use from the 8th December in the completely re-modelled and re-seated auditorium with its smart new proscenium, and for the first time, electrically-operated curtains. The exterior was also subject to a facelift and a new canopy provided.

No further changes took place until the installation of a wall-to-wall CinemaScope screen in 1955, by which time seating accommodation had been reduced from 450 to 384. Because of lack of support and rising overheads the closure of the Court Cinema in October 1958 was inevitable. The Director, Mr. H. Neck explained that the Directors had themselves not drawn any money since acquiring the Court and the Royal, and the two buildings had existed hand-to-mouth for some time. He mentioned the possibility of re-opening the Court the following Easter and indeed this came to pass in July 1959 with an emphasis on comedy films under the management of Messrs. A.T. Johnson and T.J. Gaffey. Surprisingly the Court continued in business for another decade closing in March 1969 with William Holden's *The Devil's Brigade*. Since then, problems with damp rot spreading to adjacent properties caused the owners to completely strip the interior of the building which then existed as an empty shell. In July 1988 Wirral magistrates made an order against George Wilkie and Co. Ltd., that the building be made safe or demolished within twenty-eight days and this resulted in demolition taking place soon afterwards.

Daylight Cinema

On Saturday the 10th May 1913, Wallasey's most unusual cinema opened adjacent to the Tower Grounds amusement complex, with Messrs. Pike and Alcock as leasees. Under an awning in a sheltered position of Quarry Gardens by the promenade, a collection of deck chairs and benches provided seating accommodation for several hundred people. The screen was positioned on a platform that was also used by variety artistes who performed to fill in gaps as film reels were being changed. The projectionist and his equipment were housed in a wooden tower-like structure behind the audience. This was the first location in this part of the UK to offer such entertainment.

It was claimed that the pictures were produced using a novel process to enable them to be distinct when projected onto the screen in daylight. First class pictures and variety entertainment was advertised twice daily at 3.00 and 8.00 p.m. with prices ranging from 3d to 1/-. Despite the claims for bright and clear pictures the same could not be guaranteed for the New Brighton weather which, no doubt, was in part the impetus for the early demise of this venture at the end of the following July.

Daylight cinema (1913)

DAYLIGHT CINEMA.

QUARRY GARDENS,
PROMENADE, NEW BRIGHTON.

—

FIRST-CLASS PICTURE AND VARIETY ENTERTAINMENT.

OPENS TO-DAY. SATURDAY.

10TH INST.

—

PERFORMANCES TWICE DAILY at 3 and 8.

—

POPULAR PRICES—3d., 6d, and 1s

Gaumont

After the Lyceum was destroyed by fire in 1932 the ruins were demolished to make way for the new Gaumont at the corner of King Street and Trafalgar Road, Egremont. Interestingly, during the site-clearing operation a number of artifacts were unearthed including coins, documents and old newspapers. These had been buried in 1862 when the foundation stone was laid for the Presbyterian Church, the predecessor to the Lyceum.

The Gaumont, the town's most luxurious cinema, opened in the presence of the Mayor of Wallasey, Councillor Henry J. Hall JP on Monday the 13th of November 1933, with a showing of *I Was A Spy* made with a mammoth cast, including Conrad Veidt and Madeleine Carroll. The supporting programme consisted of Laurel and Hardy in *Towed in a Hole*, the Mickey Mouse cartoon, *Building a Building, The Gaumont Mirror* and the latest news in *The Gaumont Graphic*.

Originally, it had been planned to construct a conventional type of theatre with balcony, but it was discovered that 'ancient lights' of adjoining buildings would be infringed upon. In order to overcome this problem the design was changed to that of a stadium style cinema with a stepped circle area at the rear of the auditorium.

Architecturally, the new building, designed by Mr. W.E. Trent, was of classical style and the outward appearance was described as being restrained and dignified. It relied for effect on a few decorative details to contrast with the simplicity of the main fabric of the building. Thus, the exterior frontage of the cinema was of brick and artificial stone dressing, brilliantly illuminated and with a well-lit canopy stretching across the three main entrances. Above the three main windows were semi-circular carved panels of stone designed by the Gaumont-British Corporation's artist, Mr. F. Barnes, to symbolise the production, projection and presentation stages of the movies.

Gaumont (1933)

Staff at the Gaumont Palace (November 1933)

Gaumont Palace (1933)

The entrance hall itself was lined with horizontal panels of Italian and French walnut surmounted by frieze of attractively grained "curly" birch. Three large diamond-shaped light fittings in the colourful and ornate ceiling lit the hall, and in keeping with the luxury cinemas of the day, the foyer was both large and rich in design. From the entrance hall one passed into the 60 ft. long lounge, which was essentially modern in its decorative treatment with a feeling of intricacy imparted by the various surfaces of the walls and ceilings and the richness of their colourings. An unusual feature was the long continuous row of tubular light fittings along the centre of the ceiling leading the eye towards the entrance to the auditorium at each end of the lounge.

The general style of the auditorium was one of warmth and 'horizontality'. The latter resulted from a combination of its vast width of over 70 ft., the relatively low ceiling for this size of cinema, coupled with the emphasised perspective caused by the ceiling beams, ribs, cornices and enriched bands etc. which all tended to converge on the 40 ft. wide proscenium as the focal point. As mentioned earlier no balcony was provided and the seating capacity of 1,209 was composed of 777 seats in the stalls and a further 432 seats on the raised platform at the rear of the hall. The main upper-part of the walls was covered in a richly coloured modern tapestry which was manufactured in Birkenhead and which served both as a decorative feature and as an acoustical aid. Below this the deep blue dado complemented the upholstery and carpets. Lighting was provided by wall lights, each comprising columns of glass cylinders mounted in trios on vermillion rods which projected at an angle beyond the face of the walls to provide a necessary contrasting member to the general horizontality of the decorative scheme. The main auditorium illumination came from two rows of

Gaumont Palace (1933)

Gaumont Palace (1933)

concealed lighting and eight large ceiling-fittings. Additional lighting coves above the proscenium and two-colour lighting were provided to enhance the appearance of the two decorative grilles in the side walls at either side of the proscenium, and also to illuminate in contrasting colours the ribbed fibrous plaster work of the coves flanking the stage, all serving to supplement the main lighting system.

The stage itself was 9 ft. in depth and was equipped with three-colour circuit footlights together with an overhead batten operated by a dimmer attached to the screen curtain controller. The main curtain was of heavy velour in a rich reddish-brown colour to harmonise with the main colouring of the walls. At the bottom edge was a deep fringe in gold and the curtains were backed with a special fire proofed material. Two sets of leg curtains and borders were provided in material that once again harmonised with the general decorative treatment of the theatre whilst the electrically-driven screen curtains were in a light neutral coloured material which was enhanced by a design along the lower edge in deep blue. As the main curtains were operated by a hand winch at the side of the stage, it was the practice for one of the projectionists to start opening these curtains about five minutes before the performance commenced and this operation would provide a focus of attention for the audience, watching the heavy curtains opening ever so slowly up to the time when the house lights dimmed for the commencement of the show. Another unusual feature at the Gaumont Palace was the provision of a 'non-sync' room beneath the front of the stage, where a dual turntable record reproducer was situated as a source of musical entertainment before the show and during intervals. There was even a special member of staff employed to do this job, referred to as 'the non-sync girl'. She wore a similar uniform to that of the usherettes, but was under the control of the chief projectionist and could only be called upon to do usherette duties at times of dire necessity. It was therefore her job during the time when films were being shown to take up a position at the very rear of the auditorium where special controls were provided for her to adjust sound levels. This situation lasted up till 1939 when staffing economies brought about relocation of the 'non-sync' to its more conventional position in the projection room. The projectors at the Gaumont Palace, incidentally, were G.B. Kalee machines with British Acoustic Sound equipment, and it is said that the opening of the theatre was nearly delayed through the addressing of the sound equipment to Egremont in Cumberland. A slide lantern and spotlight, together with automatic dimmers for the house lights and manual dimmers for the colour lighting round the proscenium, completed the projection room equipment. An organ chamber was provided but, alas, no organ.

Matinees were daily at 2.30 p.m. and evening performances continuous from 6.15 p.m. Prices were 1/3, 9d and 7d with reductions for matinees. The staff of nearly thirty was headed by Fred J. Smidmore, formerly of the Trocadero, Liverpool. In keeping with many up-market picture houses of the period, such as the Ritz in Birkenhead a few years later, much was made of the uniform worn by the staff. The usherettes were dressed in dark red with navy facing and collars, whilst the doormen wore black uniforms with gold braid and white gloves. Mr. Smidmore was not to remain long at Wallasey, leaving a year later to open the new Gaumont Palace at Derby. His place at Wallasey was then taken by Henry Gurney, a former manager at the Lyceum, who was to become a well-known and well-liked manager for some years to come. It was he who introduced popular Sunday concerts at the Gaumont Palace for the winter season, commencing from the 26th December 1937. The bands featured were usually local groups, as well as those employed at G.B.-operated ballrooms in the north of England, such as that of Bob Easson from the Rialto in Liverpool, but sometimes bands such as that of Larry Brennan from the Empress Ballroom in Blackpool appeared. The Sunday concerts were once nightly and were resumed again, after a break during the summer season, in September 1938, and then again from October 1939 when among the bands featured was one conducted by Henry Croudson, the organist from the Ritz, Birkenhead.

The introduction of Sunday cinemas to Wallasey brought an end to stage concerts at the Gaumont Palace, but the theatre continued to be one of Wallasey's most popular venues for entertainment right into the early 1950's. In October 1954 a new wide screen was installed at the front of the stage and the first CinemaScope Film, *The Black Shield of Falworth*, was screened in December of that year. However, these innovations did nothing to halt the then declining attendances and in 1967 the theatre was one of those sold by Rank to the expanding Classic circuit. The theatre was then re-named Classic but a

WALLASEY GAUMONT

PROGRAMMES

further decline in attendances caused the new owners to introduce bingo for a short period early in 1969 with films only being shown on a Sunday and at the Saturday morning children's show. To facilitate bingo, the stage was extended forward and the footlights removed, but in April 1969 there was a reversion to full-time cinema programmes. The next bingo threat came in September 1973 when the owners of the nearby Royal Bingo Club agreed to take over the Classic providing that a new bingo licence could be obtained, the former licence having lapsed in the meantime. Opposition to this was organised by one of the present authors and finally, by a margin of one vote, the council turned down the bingo application.

The next change came when Unit Four Cinemas of Burnley took over the cinema in October 1974 to offer a 300% increase in the choice of films to its patrons. A potential advantage of this arrangement was the possibility of attracting family visitors when children could attend one Unit whilst their parents watched films in one of the adjoining cinemas. Within weeks of the take-over, Unit Four set about splitting the auditorium into four separate cinemas. The stalls area was sub-divided into three cinemas with a new projection room sited above the aisle that formerly divided the stalls from the circle. The fourth cinema was in the circle area using the original projection facilities. In 1979 an additional £80,000 was spent over a two month period on further sub-division of the former circle and the installation of two extra screens, (making a total of six cinemas in the complex). Despite this change, the picture house was still referred to as 'Unit Four'. The original lounge now houses a licensed bar and facilities for advance bookings were provided. This cinema complex, together with the modified Pheonix, was the first multiple cinema in Wirral. The catchment area was targeted further afield than just local residents as data suggested that 53% of customers travelled to the cinema by car.

Although the cinema has survived as the only picture-house in Wallasey, and indeed one of the few existing cinemas on the Wirral, it is unfortunate that no vestige of the former grandeur of the Gaumont Palace now remains. The new screens have no curtains other than those used to cover the hardboard dividing walls, the beautiful light fittings have been consigned to the scrap heap, and the opulent wood panelling in the entrance hall has now been covered by orange emulsion paint. What a sad end for Wallasey's luxury cinema!

Hales Tours Of The World

July 1907 saw the opening of a novel form of cinema in the Tower Grounds. This was of American origin. Patrons sat inside a representation of a spacious railway saloon-car in which panoramic scenery effects were produced by a cinematograph to produce the illusion of movement, and the views were described by the conductor. The car was said to rock, sway and jolt, wheels rumble, and engine-whistle shrieks could be heard as the 'train' traversed bridges and dashed through cuttings in Africa and the North American continent. Indeed one could 'travel' around the world in ten minutes. The ornate complex, but compact structure, was erected in fourteen days and was under the superintendance of Mr. W. Yates Gregory. The performances lasted throughout the summer season of 1907, but were not repeated in subsequent years at New Brighton, although other versions were installed at Manchester, Leeds, Halifax, Margate, Dublin and Glasgow.

TOWER,
NEW BRIGHTON.
Manager .... WILLIAM HOLLAND.

TO-Day, at 3.30 and 8.
Enormous success of the Grand Production of JOHN
TILLER'S COMPANY, the Topsy-Bateau Comedy
Extravaganza The

ALABAMA COON.

BER BIRTHDAY,
A Short Ballet Divertisement.

FREE FUN PARK.

ABYSSINIAN VILLAGE,

HALE'S TOURS OF THE WORLD
NOW OPEN.

WAGNER CONCERT

H ALE'S T OURS
OF THE W ORLD

PULLMAN CARS RUN
EVERY FEW MINUTES,
FROM THE
T OWER G ROUNDS,
N EW B RIGHTON.

A TRIP TO
PINES,
PEAK,
COLORADO,

FARES 6D. CHILDREN HALF-PRICE.

Irving Theatre

(Kings/La Scala/Hippodrome/Embassy)

The Irving Theatre situated in Victoria Road (later to become Borough Road), Seacombe, was a typical ornate Edwardian theatre. It was built on a site previously occupied by Hope House and its gardens, for Mr. James Kiernan as part of his growing empire of theatres. The distinguished actor Sir Henry Irving laid the cornerstone of the building on 11th October 1899 and agreed for his name to be associated with the building for as long as it was used for serious theatre as opposed to music-hall entertainment. After the laying ceremony a recherche luncheon was held in honour of Sir Henry's visit at the Seacombe Ferry Hotel, at which Sir Edward Russell presided. The grand opening took place on Monday 18th December 1899 with a performance of *The Sign Of The Cross* by a cast of over sixty performers. Mr. J.H. French became the manager and soon after opening, this "Temple of Thesbus" was granted a liquor licence.

The auditorium consisted of stalls and a steeply stepped horse-shoe shaped balcony that was supported by six pillars. Seating was provided for over 900. At either side of the stage were two tiers of boxes and the stage itself was fully equipped with fly-tower and could handle the most elaborate productions.

After refurbishment work in 1904, which included re-flooring the pit, laying linoleum, installing new seats and putting up a draught screen in the stalls, the theatre re-opened in September and film shows were introduced as part of the programme. This was the first opportunity for Wallasey's 80,000 inhabitants to see the new wonder of the age which was billed as the main attraction rather than as a subsidiary part of a variety show. The opening programme on Monday the 12th of September, was advertised as "The Rage of Liverpool! Animated Picture World" and featured animated pictures of the Royal Visit to Liverpool and "the greatest collection of living pictures the world has ever produced", including LIVING WALLASEY from day to day incidents taken from real life. Also included were *Off For The Holidays, Pictures from Lakeland to the Isle of Man,* and *The Miser's Daughter*, plus shots of the Russo-Japan war. Picture quality was advertised as "No flickering! Bright, Brilliant and Clear". The Empire Comedy Quintette, the Monte Carlo Duettists, Alf Poynton (Actor and Drawing Room Entertainer) and Thos. Shaw's Celebrated Orchestra, all

Irving Theatre (1906)

Ludwig Blattner conducting the orchestra at the Irving

provided the supporting live entertainment. A wide variety of seats were available with admission charges of Boxes 21/-, 10/-, 3/- and 2/6; Orchestra Stalls 2/-; Dress Circle 1/6; Pit Stalls 1/-; Family Circle 1/-; Pit; 6d and Gallery 4d. There was one performance nightly at 8.00 p.m.

Simultaneously with the showing of animated pictures in Wallasey, performances at the Picton Hall were publicised in the local press and a coupon printed in the 'Wallasey News' enabled readers to claim 6d rebate on their entrance fee towards the cost of their ferry and tram fares to Liverpool.

Several seasons of films followed the opening performance, in each case supported by songs and other live entertainment including Grand Diabolo competitions and 'Go-as-you-please' concerts. In 1908 a serious fire in the theatre closed the building for several months causing £2,000 damage. Soon after re-opening, music hall programmes were re-introduced which, because of the personal agreement with Irving, necessitated a change in the name of the establishment, this time to the Kings Theatre.

During the next twenty five years or so the premises experienced several closures, refurbishments, changes in management and in name, and its use oscillated between that of a cinema and live theatre. Thus, after a period of closure for extensive re-decoration and renovation, it re-opened on Easter Monday 1912 under the management of Ludwig Blattner and it became known as 'La Scala — The Philharmonic Cinema'. By now the building had been fitted throughout with tip-up seats, had been re-carpeted and the stage was draped with red velvet curtains whilst variegated plants adorned the orchestra pit. The person responsible for these changes was the talented German manager himself. Even the New Cosmopolitan Orchestra was conducted by Blattner, often playing his own compositions including a waltz entitled *Ladies of Wallasey*, claimed to be popular with cinema orchestras throughout the land. Once again the film season was followed by a reversion to purely stage shows and by 1914 a new manager was at the helm. The theatre closed for extensive re-decoration and renovation in 1918 before re-opening later the same year as the Hippodrome under the management of Mr. F.V. Ross, who was also the manager of the Tivoli Theatre in New Brighton. Films featured once again in 1921 with a 'Repertoire Picture Season' during which period a different film was shown each night and music was provided by "An orchestra worthy of the name under the leadership of the masked conductor". The Hippodrome however reverted to stage shows later in the year, a style of entertainment which became the main bill of fare throughout the 1920's, albeit with further changes in administration, as in 1928 when the Gordon Circuit acquired the theatre and spent £1,500 on improvements.

Embassy views of entrance hall before and after reconstruction in 1938

Business at the Hippodrome declined at the start of the following decade and throughout most of 1932 the theatre remained closed. The re-opening on Boxing Day that year under the management of C.W.F. Bruton, was short lived and the premises closed again in April the following year. A final attempt to make the Hippodrome pay as a theatre was made in 1934 under the ownership of Pat Collins and management of Dick Batchelor. This team had the building renovated and re-decorated and introduced a new seven-piece orchestra with Ben Parks as director. The diagnosis of the problem proved to be inept and final closure as a theatre came on 27th April after plans to re-open in August with a new stage never materialised.

When the building did re-open, it was on Monday 20th April 1936 as the Embassy Luxury Theatre with Harry Buxton as owner (also proprietor of the Picturedrome in Birkenhead) and R.A. Morton Martin as manager. At last, cine

Embassy views of auditorium before and after reconstruction in 1938

variety had come to Wallasey and the Mayor of Wallasey, Mr. A.W. Vicory Stoins, who was presented with a cheque for the Wallasey Children's Holiday Home at Ellesmere, performed the opening ceremony at the entirely re-decorated theatre. In the auditorium there were new seats in the circle, including many 'twin' seats, and the creation of a beautiful mottled effect achieved by the application of 'scientific' spray painting and use throughout of new lighting of modern design. The futuristic atmosphere was extended into the entrance hall by use of artistic glazing and mirrors. The cinema screen was set well back on the stage in order that the variety shows could be staged in front of it, and three sets of reversible 'leg' and 'border' curtains were provided, one side being in deep red velour, and the other green, so that stage settings could be varied. Back-drops and scenery were sometimes used for stage shows.

The opening performance lasted for two hours thirty minutes and featured Robert Donat and Jean Parker on screen in *The Ghost Goes West*. On stage were Syd Mack and his Broadcasting Band; the BBC star Maggie Stott (The Singing Mill Girl); Ralphono — The Great Conjuror; and the 12 Alhambra Kiddies billed as The World's Most Talented Juveniles. Entrance charges were 6d, 1/- and 1/3.

Subsequent cine-variety programmes included *Captain Villiers Great Television Show* and weekly Amateur Talent Contests. But despite these attractions the theatre was once again up for sale later in the year. Then North Western Cinemas, proprietors of the Liscard Palace and the Liverpool Palais de Luxe, took over and announced that from 26th September 1936 the theatre would be used solely as a cinema. At this time admission was 1/- in the circle and 6d for the stalls with entrance to the 2.30 p.m. matinees at half price.

One year later to the month, further changes were made to the Embassy. These included the use of a new lighting system claimed to be the first of its type in the North of England. This was the new system "Holophane auto-selective system", which had been installed on the stage and in the auditorium and enabled three colours to be blended so as to create any of the colours of the spectrum. In addition to the footlights, lighting battens were also strategically placed at the side of the stage and above to illuminate the new fully-festooned silver satin screen curtains. Further lighting was also used in the curtained-off boxes at the side of the stage, and the latest B.T.H. system was installed to provide high-fidelity sound reproduction.

Even so, by far the most striking changes to this building occurred in 1938, when after a three month period of closure, the Embassy underwent a metamorphosis both externally and internally. The auditorium had been completely re-constructed on a modern approach; the bottle-neck shaped configuration had given way to a new fan-shaped auditorium in which the side walls followed a wide curve into a simple stage surround, the ante-proscenium being thrown into prominence by a horizontal grille treatment terminated by the flanking pillars of the proscenium. The ornate ceiling had been replaced with a more modern version that swept down in a series of curves towards the stage with coves which ingeniously concealed lighting to illuminate the futuristic painted designs that were a feature of both ceiling and walls. In order to improve the view the old horse-shoe balcony with its supporting pillars had been replaced by a large new balcony supported by the side walls of the building. The entrance hall had also been completely remodelled with a new pay-box recessed into the wall. The heating and ventilation systems were also up-graded.

Outwardly too, the front of the exterior was also given a new image which was achieved by a modern canopy and vitrolite cladding in cream, green and black applied to the lower part of the frontage.

At long last and after such a chequered history, the old Irving Theatre had become a commercially viable cinema and it continued under the ownership of North Western Cinemas without further alterations up to the second half of the century. In June 1955 a new wide screen for CinemaScope was installed closer to the front of the stage and new festoon curtains surrounded by only one set of 'legs' with matching border were provided. But sadly just four years later Mr. Hector McQueen, supervisor of the North Western Cinema Circuit, announced the closure of the Embassy (the fifth cinema in Wallasey to close). The cause was attributed to the depression and over twenty members of staff were affected. The final film was Richard Attenborough and John Gregson in *Sea of Sand*. Since its closure the premises have been used for bingo whilst the balcony was used for a short while as a separate night club.

Embassy auditorium after reconstruction in 1938

*Embassy view of exterior before and after
reconstruction in 1938*

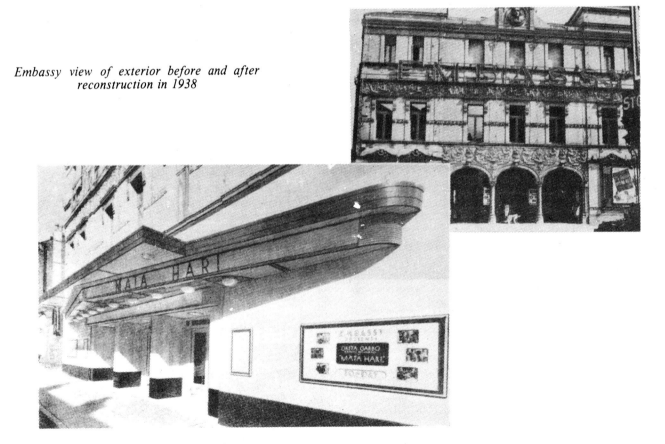

Liscard Electric Palace

On 25th November 1911, just three weeks after the opening of the Queens, Wallasey's second purpose-built cinema, The Liscard Electric Palace, opened in Seaview Road in the centre of the town. This proved to be one of Wallasey's best lov. ' cinemas.

The main entrance was flanked by two shops and surmounted by a large glass canopy below an elaborate and dazzling white, fibrous plaster-covered facade that included three arched window features and, like the Queens, was illuminated at night by hundreds of lights. The spacious and handsomely decorated entrance hall with its marble floor was relieved with delightfully coloured windows. The main paybox was on the right hand side of the vestibule and a feature of the entrance hall was the centrally located kiosk from which refreshments could be purchased. Two broad luxuriously carpeted staircases led to the small 180 seater grand circle. The golden panelling of the walls artistically harmonised with the coloured lights. The windows near the top of the building dispensed with any need for artificial lighting during the day.

The rather narrow auditorium was capable of holding a total audience of 700 and curtains enclosing the entrance doors eliminated most of the draughts on the ground floor. Both the screen and the stage were tastefully encased in moulded design whilst the side walls between the pilasters were adorned with a series of panels framed in heavy plaster mouldings. The pilasters themselves were decorated with medallions in bas-relief. Further elaborate touches were provided in the auditorium by the deep dado with heavy moulded capping and an attractive colour scheme in which yellow predominated and which was finished with pairs of warm red coloured flambeaux wall lights on the pilasters. The majority of ground floor exits opened on to a passage at the right hand side of the building that was also used as a separate entrance to the front stalls area.

Liscard Palace (1935)

Staff from the Liscard Electric Palace (1930's)

The opening programme was billed as "World in Action Animated Photograph: interspersed with vocal items". The films shown included *Mount Etna in Eruption, Gay Time in Washington, Circular Fence, Italian Blood, Parson and the Bully, Woman in Town, Three Brothers* and *Beware of the Dog*. Evening performances were continuous from 6.30 to 10.30 p.m. and there were matinees daily at 3.00 p.m. at which afternoon tea was served free. Prices were Pit stalls 3d, Stalls 6d and Grand Balcony 1/-. The manager at the time was Reginald F. Astley who was later succeeded by Claude Adams who remained in charge for many years.

After the initial opening of the Liscard Palace there were several important milestones in the history of this cinema worthy of recording. Thus in 1920 the screen end of the premises was extended and the seating capacity increased to just under a thousand. Two years later the two shops were incorporated into the cinema to provide waiting room accommodation. In January 1923 *The Glorious Adventure*, advertised as the first colour picture to be made in England, was shown. It was produced in 'Natural Colour' which was said to be "rather too sharply defined at times rather gaudy". As part of a redecoration scheme in 1928 the panels on the side walls were painted with attractive murals depicting Venetian and Swiss scenes, whilst at the screen end of the hall bottle-green velour curtains trimmed with gold were put up together with 'swags' in matching material. On 4th August 1930 when B.T.H. sound had been installed Marion Davies featured in her "talking and singing triumph", 'Marianne', the first sound picture to be shown at the Palace. In 1931, the Universal British Talking News with commentary by R.E. Jeffrey, the world-famous BBC commentator, was a popular addition to every programme.

On 15th June 1935 it was announced that the Liscard Palace would close for one week for modernisation and decoration, during which time a complete transformation of the auditorium was to take place. All the old fibrous plaster treatment was removed from the side walls and the latest form of modernistic decoration was applied using echo resisting plastic paint. Beautiful shades of greens, creams, pinks, Venetian reds and silver giving a rich colourful atmosphere were applied, whilst the ceiling panels were painted in varying shades of blue, the darkest shades being adjacent to the screen. At either side of the new proscenium were ornate ventilation grilles and the theatre was reseated throughout with the latest sorbo-padded 'bucket' seats; new projection equipment and improved sound were also provided. ·

Some of the most noticeable changes to the Palace were at the screen end of the building where a new, shallow, stage platform had been constructed and fitted out with two sets of curtains. The main drapery was in gold appliqued with a bold pattern in brilliant coloured silks, and was operated by a hand winch in the projection room. The screen curtains, which were electrically operated, were fully festooned in silver satin with a trio of panels per curtain. The *piece de resistance* however, was the Holophane auto-cycle colour lighting that illuminated these curtains in ever-changing hues through the medium of footlights, an overhead batten and vertical battens at either side of the stage. After all this grandeur the film must have seemed an anti-climax!

The cinema continued to draw crowds right into the 1950's when the Liscard Palace also began to experience the general trend of declining box-office takings. At the start of this decade the original but crumbling facade was replaced with a new rustic brick version, and in 1955 a new 30ft wide CinemaScope screen was placed forward of the original proscenium and an upward-rising festoon curtain was installed. However, this did little to relieve the recession and *Love Slaves of the Amazon* with Don Taylor and Gia Segale plus *Hold Back Tomorrow* with Cleo Moore and John Agar shown on 3rd June 1959 were the last two films screened at the Palace. The manager at the time was Mr. S. Wynn who explained the reason for closing was due to falling support; the staff of twelve were made redundant. Following the closure of the Embassy and the Winter Gardens, the Palace was the third cinema to close in Wallasey that year.

The building was then converted into a Lennon's supermarket, and at the moment is a shoe supermarket.

Liscard Palace prior to conversion into a supermarket (1962)

The Lyceum Electric Palace

In 1908 the congregation of the Presbyterian Church in King Street, Egremont, moved to new premises and the vacated building remained dormant for a couple of years before its potential as a picture house was realised. The new proprietors, The Perfect Projection Picture Company, opened the building as the Lyceum at the beginning of 1910 for a brief period under the management of Mr. E. Gray.

Lyceum Electric Palace (1920's)

As a result of its ecclesiastic pedigree the Lyceum was an inspiring building, the frontage of which resembled a Roman Temple with its stone steps leading up to the main entrance and the six Tuscan Doric columns supporting an entablature with pediment and tympanum. A glazed canopy which was constructed around the columns, covered the full width of the entrance. A patron of the cinema in the early days, however, remembers that despite the grandeur of the facade, inside the church pews were still in existence for some time on the ground floor, and because the floor was not raked, it was necessary for the screen to be placed quite high up on the rear wall of the hall to ensure that the audience would have an unimpeded view. An unfortunate aspect of this arrangement was the fact that the front stalls patrons usually left the picture house suffering from a stiff neck! The projection room was at the front of the building at the rear of the balcony. The earliest advertised films included *Silent Watches of the Night*, described as "an American dramatic enactment which is shown with especial clearness and steadiness, and calls for rapturous applause". In addition to the films, a Miss Eva Carter was said to be "warmly and deservedly encored for her baritone contributions to the programme".

The building had a chequered history from the time it opened, undergoing a series of modification and changes in management and it experienced its share of misfortune. Indeed at the onset the manager had promised to transform the historic structure into one of the most comfortable houses in the district. The first improvements came later in 1910 after a period of closure. The Lyceum Electric Palace re-opened on August Bank Holiday at 2.00 p.m. with a film of the Chester Pageant and "The Latest Picture Novelties". Admission was: 'Area' 3d and Balcony 6d, with charges for children at 2d and 3d. Performances were continuous from 6.00 till 10.30 p.m. on weekdays and from 2.00 p.m. on Saturdays and holidays. Films were changed twice weekly. Much of the interior had now been reconstructed and redecorated to provide capacity for 600 patrons in more comfortable surroundings. In the auditorium the supporting columns and the side galleries had been removed. New seats were installed and the five deep arched church windows had been bricked in. It was now advertised as "Absolutely the most magnificent place of amusement in the provinces" and an added attraction from 24th September was the New Bijou Orchestra under Mr. Bescoby who later became director of the Trocadero Symphony Orchestra, New Brighton.

LYCEUM

KING STREET.

TALKIES——TALKIES.

British Acoustic Sound System—

Embodying all the Very Latest Improvements.

MONDAY, 1st SEPT.—For 3 Days Only.

Grand All-Talking Opening Attraction.

ELINOR GLYN'S STORY—

"SUCH MEN ARE DANGEROUS."

Starring

WARNER BAXTER and **CATHERINE DALE OWEN.**

THURSDAY, FRIDAY, SATURDAY—

RICARDO CORTEZ & NANCY WELFORD

in the 100 per cent. Dialogue Mystery thriller—

"THE PHANTOM IN THE HOUSE."

Also **CARMEN BONI** in

"LATIN QUARTER."

Accompanied by the Lyceum Orchestra.

**Evenings—Circle 1/-; Stalls 8d., Pit 6d.
Matinee Daily—Circle 6d., Stalls 3d.**

Further improvements were described in May 1911 when a "new and complete system of ventilation" was added to "the prettiest picture palace in the district". The theatre was now under the management of a Matthew Raymond who also conducted the orchestra and provided vocal interludes between the films, these songs sometimes being illustrated with slides. The entrance hall now boasted rich red plain carpeting with slim brass stair-rods on the staircases at either side with bronze balustrades. The entrance doors were fully glazed with bevelled glass panels and there was an ornate central mahogany paybox office with gilt lining. Opaque glass bowl light fittings completed the scheme.

The lofty-ceilinged auditorium had recessed panels along the walls where the deep church windows had formerly been, and there was now a slightly raked floor in the stalls. An orchestra pit and small platform were provided in front of the stage and chandelier lights with pink-tinged shades were hung from the ceiling with matching light fittings mounted on the walls.

In the next few years ownership of the Lyceum (often referred to by patrons as 'The Lyce') changed hands first to Bedford Cinemas in the early 1920's and then to the Gaumont-British Picture Corporation in 1928. Plans announced two years later to replace the Lyceum with a more palatial building came to nothing. British Acoustic sound equipment was installed at the end of the summer 1930 and the first talkie at the Lyceum on the 1st September 1930 was *Such Men are Dangerous* featuring Warren Baxter and Catherine Dale Owen.

In the early 1930's the Lyceum suffered from a series of fires. The first outbreak at the end of 1930 involved a small fire in a store room which caused minimal damage, but a second fire five months later resulted in closure of the balcony until August. The Lyceum was again in the news on the 18th August 1931 when the wife of the chief projectionist, E.F. Whitman was killed in a tragic bus accident. (Mr. Whitman had been with his wife on a shopping expedition to Liverpool on his afternoon off and returned on the ferry boat that connected with the 5 o'clock bus from Seacombe Ferry. The bus was one of a fleet of six-wheel Karrier vehicles that had replaced trams on the route that passed the Lyceum a few years earlier, and as it slowed down to stop outside the theatre the drive shaft suddenly broke away from its mountings and was forced up through the floor at the very moment when Mrs. Whitman was walking down the centre aisle towards the rear platform. The unfortunate woman was dragged through the floor of the bus and her body was deposited on the road beneath the vehicle. The funeral took place the following week and was attended by representatives from all the Borough's cinemas).

The final disaster struck in the early hours of 30th December 1931 when, just twelve months after the first fire, a more major fire broke out. A passer-by reported flames leaping through the theatre windows but desite valiant efforts by the Wallasey Fire Brigade the auditorium was completely destroyed and only the projection suite at the front of the building with its equipment and films survived the blaze. The Lyceum was pulled down in March 1933 to make way for the Gaumont Palace.

Fire damage/demolition at the Lyceum

Marina

The Marina Super Cinema, designed by A. Ernest Shennan of Liverpool, was situated in Brighton Street on the site formerly occupied by the Vienna Hall which had closed the previous year. It was opened by the Mayor of Wallasey Alderman Sidney S. Pawson, on 15th July 1916 with the feature film *The Second Mrs. Tanqueray* starring Sir George Alexander and Miss Hilda Moor. Music was provided by a 'Symphony Orchestra' comprising two violins, a cello and a double bass under the direction of Alfred Delmonte at the piano. Proceeds from the opening performance were donated to the Mayor's fund. Matinees were daily at 3.00 p.m. with continuous performances from 6.30 to 10.30 p.m. Seating capacity was 950 and the owners were Bedford Cinemas Ltd., of Liverpool the resident manager being Alfred E. Brewer previously with the Palais de Luxe, Liverpool.

Marina (1916)

MARINA, THE SUPER CINEMA, BRIGHTON-STREET, SEACOMBE.

GRAND OPENING TO-DAY, BY THE MAYOR OF WALLASEY (ALDERMAN SIDNEY S, DAWSON, J.P.)

CONTINUOUS PERFORMANCE - 6-30 to 10-30. ENTIRE PROCEEDS TO THE MAYOR'S FUND.

MONDAY, TUESDAY, and WEDNESDAY.

SIR GEORGE ALEXANDER AND MISS HILDA MOORE IN

THE SECOND MRS. TANQUERAY.

MATINEE DAILY AT 3. CONTINUOUS PERFORMANCE 6-30 to 10-30 P.M.

The attractive frontage with its red-glazed bricks had a flight of white marble steps surmounted by a large bronze ornamental canopy leading up to the four entrance doors which had diamond-shaped bevelled glass panels. There was a narrow vestibule with black and white patterned marble floors leading into the red-carpeted entrance hall with its pay-box facing the entrance. The staircases at either side leading to the balcony were also carpeted in red and had large brass stair rods matching the heavy brass hand rails, door pulls and crash bars. Lighting in the foyer was provided by a large multiple bowl Electrolier.

The auditorium had a lofty ceiling and the panels betweeen the pilasters on the side walls were decorated with dark patterned wallpaper, above which three small rectangular windows were provided immediately below the deep cornice, and there was a dark wood panelled dado. The floor was not very steeply raked and therefore the screen was a considerable height from the floor, being painted on the rear wall and surrounded by a fibrous plaster frame. The small, but commodious balcony had a concave front and a seating capacity for 220. The main auditorium lighting was provided by single bowl off-white opaque glass Electroliers suspended on long brass chains from copper rims.

In 1928 the Marina became a Gaumont-British theatre and on 21st April 1930 the British Acoustic Sound Reproducing System had been installed for the Marina's first talkie, *The Sky Hawk*, a Movietone romance with John Garrick, Helen Chandler and Gilbert Emery. There were no further changes at the Marina until June 1955 when a new wide screen was fitted and in March of the following year the theatre was completely redecorated. However, closure came suddenly on 22nd September 1956 with the last film being Kenneth Moore in *Reach for the Sky*. After this the Marina lay derelict until the 1970's when demolition took place to make way for extensions to a nearby school.

Marina (1960s)

Moreton Picture House

Plans for the Moreton Picture House were presented to the local magistrates by Mr. S.F. Moor on behalf of Mr. William Wainwright and approved in August 1919. The cinema, designed by A.E. Shennan who was later responsible for designing some of Merseyside's most opulent picture-houses such as the Plaza in Birkenhead, was built on more modest grounds at 16 Station Road (later renamed Pasture Road), Moreton for Cheshire Picture Halls. This company already owned the Palladium, Coliseum, Empire and Lyceum. It was a rather cheaply built cinema, adopting the Tudor style with half timbered frontage (and indeed was known as Ye Olde English Picture House) with a canopy supported by two piers between which were two shops. It had accommodation for around 850 in total. The inside plan was typical of the period. The seats were upholstered in rich crimson and blue velvet. Access to the balcony, which was described as graceful, was from the entrance hall via two marble staircases balustraded with hand-wrought iron work. The lights were classed as a striking feature. The operators room was commodious and was cut off from the audience by automatic iron doors. The quality of the pictures was described as being so good as not to cause eye strain, and the ventilation of the building was up to date to add to the hygiene of the premises. During the construction, two changes were made to the original plans. Firstly, it was initially intended to house the generating room in a basement but the land proved to be too water logged and an external annexe was provided. Secondly, the plans showed a sloping side passage but this was eventually levelled thereby obviating the need for steps.

Moreton Picture House
(1920's)

The cinema was officially opened on 30th April 1921 and the first film to be shown was *Wit Wins* and the manager was Mr. W.W. Wright. At the time Moreton was a largely unbuilt area and the people of Wallasey would pass through when making excursions to the rural parts beyond. The appeal of the cinema, therefore, was targeted not only at the local populace but also to those from the surrounding district "fond of a cycle trip" and who would "welcome the opportunity of breaking their homeward journey at Moreton for a short respite with entertainment". Indeed free storage was provided for cycles. The price of seats ranged from 9d in the front stalls, 1/- for reserved stalls, and 1/7 in the balcony. There were two performances each evening at 6.40 and 8.40 with matinees at 2.45 p.m. Silent movies were advertised up until 6th October 1930 when *Two Big Vagabonds* was screened. Thereafter silents were again advertised for some time.

Cheshire Picture Halls had become part of the S. M. Super Cinemas circuit by 1937 and the Moreton Picture House continued to operate under their management until this company in turn was taken over by the Essoldo chain in 1954.

In 1957 the cinema experienced an outbreak of theft which included seating, a refrigerator, and cash. Upon investigation the culprit proved to be the cinema fireman.

The Moreton Picture House closed on 28th March 1964 with a showing of *Flight of the White Stallion* starring Robert Taylor and Lilli Palmer and since then it remains largely un-changed as a Top Flight Bingo Club.

Old Court House Picturedrome

(Kinema/Kings/Picture House/Continental)

The conversion of the old Court House in Liscard Road into a 400 seater cinema represented one of the most curious transformations of a building into a picture house in the Wirral, when one of the former basement cells came in handy to house the electric generator. The opening was first announced on Saturday 31st January 1914 when, under the management of Mr. James Burt, a full programme of 'all-star' pictures was advertised including *Her Majesty the Little Queen*. Film quality was considered to be high according to the claims for "Rock Steady Flickerless Pictures".

Performances commenced each evening at 6.30 and 10.30 p.m. with matinees at 3.00 p.m. on Wednesdays and Saturdays when free tea was served to customers. The programmes were changed twice weekly on Mondays and Thursdays, and tickets were at 3d for the Pit Stalls, 6d in the Stalls and 9d for the Balcony.

Old Court House lying derelict (1985)

Wide, steep steps led to a rather small entrance hall with its central paybox and pair of steep staircases on either side providing access to the balcony. The latter, with a front that curved sharply inwards, was relatively large in comparison with the total size of the hall and the rather cramped projection room facilities. The auditorium itself was square with a lofty ceiling and silver screen raised high up on the end wall.

These austere surroundings of the Old Court House apparently did not appeal to patrons as no further programmes were advertised between the 13th June 1914 and the autumn that year. On the 14th November 1914 the cinema, newly decorated throughout in Wedgewood style, re-opened as The Kinema under the management of C. W. Harrison. The film on this occasion was *Partners in Crime* and piano accompaniments were provided by George Briscoe. Renovations and redecorations were again reported in 1919 and next in January 1921. This latest scheme was in the style of Louis XIV with the Renaissance ornamental centre exquisitely done in oils surrounded by acanthus leaves. Wall panels were finished with orange ribbed ground and black effects whilst other decorations were in Venetian red or biscuit colour.

In 1922 an added attraction was Maurice Faust's Augmented Jazz and Symphony Band. The cinema was soon rechristened Kings and, as late as 1931, advertisements claimed "Our Silent Films Still A Big Attraction". However, the talkies finally arrived at the Kings later the same year when it appears that the apparatus broke down shortly after installation: an advertisement in the local press dated 29th August stated;

"Our Talkie Set Failed Us!!! But we will not fail our patrons. We have now installed the world's finest talkie set, 1931 latest model. Opening August 31st when we will be able to guarantee our patrons the finest, purest and clearest reproduction of any set in the district. British made and installed by British Talking Pictures Ltd.,"

Throughout the 1930's the Kings underwent several changes in management and refurbishments. A feature of the 1932 renovations was the introduction of twin seats for courting couples, whilst 1934 saw the installation of a larger screen and yet another decoration scheme. As a result of bomb blast damage during the war, the flat roof began to leak and by 1941 the general condition of the premises was dire. Cyril Bolton, the projectionist at the time, recalls a bucket and three tin baths being positioned strategically in the centre aisle to collect the water seeping through the roof on a rainy night, and indeed patrons viewing the film with their umbrellas up!

Further problems were in store for the Old Court. The lessee by this time was Arthur Bell, a gentleman from Blackpool who apparently had a drinking problem as he was frequently seen to disappear into a nearby public house after collecting the night's takings at the box office. Since there was nothing left with which to pay the bills, it wasn't long before the electricity company had disconnected the supply. A rapid visit to the electricity offices by Mr. Bell resulted in the mains being reconnected. However, there were also problems with the film renters over the supply of films which resulted in one film (the 1933 vintage Conrad Veidt film *Secrets of F.P.I.*) which was originally booked for three days having an extended run of three weeks! A notice outside stated "Retained by public demand", a claim not substantiated by the rapidly dwindling attendances. It was therefore of no surprise that in March 1942 the licensing authority refused to renew Mr. Bell's licence and a new lessee took control. Mr. Bell, clearly a bitter man, brought an action for damages against the owners of The Old Court, a Mrs. Moore, alleging that his difficulties were attributed to her failure to maintain the premises in a good state of repair. The case however, was dismissed after evidence was presented relating to Mr. Bell's record of non-payment of bills resulting in the renters' refusal to supply further films.

In May 1946, Gordon Hewart took over management and renamed the cinema The Picture House. Once again redecoration took place and for a period amateur variety shows supplemented the film programme on Tuesday and Friday evenings. By 1947 the premises were owned by Leslie Blond who also went on in 1951 to own the Phoenix (Wallasey) and in 1961 to control the Hope Hall Cinema in Liverpool. He introduced further improvements, both in terms of decor and film booking policy. Following a successful trial season of continental films in April 1949 he embarked upon a permanent policy of showing mainly foreign films at what was by then described as The Continental Picture House. The words 'Picture House' were eventually dropped from the title and The Continental was to be Merseyside's only commercial cinema specialising in foreign films right up to 1963. Closure finally came on Saturday the 2nd November 1963 with a double feature programme, *The Quare Fellow* with Patrick McGoohan and Sylvia Sims, plus *Battle of the Sexes* with Peter Sellers. The building has subsequently been used as a bingo hall but was finally demolished in 1988.

Phoenix

Phoenix (1951)

Phoenix windows of the 'cry rooms' at the back (1951)

It was not until 1951 that the post-war building restrictions were relaxed sufficiently to allow the construction of the aptly named Phoenix, which rose from the ashes of the blitzed Coliseum in Wallasey Village. The £40,000 cinema was the first to be designed by the 24 year old Liverpool architect, Mr. Alexander Webber who, four years later, went on to build the £100,000 Albany Cinema in Maghull for the same company. The design of the Albany was modelled on that of the Phoenix but with accommodation for an additional 500.

The modern Phoenix cinema was opened by the Mayor of Wallasey, Alderman G.H. Young on Monday 4th June 1951. The proprietor, Mr. Leslie Blond, described it as "A cinema of tomorrow" with equipment, amenities and design considered to be twenty years ahead of its time. The opening film was *Rio Grande* starring John Wayne and Maureen O'Hara. Admission cost 1/3, 1/10, 2/4 and 2/10 for continuous performances between 5.30 p.m. each day (from 5.00 p.m. on Sundays), and childrens' matinees at 2.00 p.m. on Saturdays.

Phoenix up for sale (1988)

The design of the building, though one of simplicity, was not without striking features. These included a pink neon Phoenix on the otherwise plain slate and rustic brick front exterior. Inside, at the extremities of the 40ft wide foyer, were the manager's office and a small buffet. All the doors were in mahogany and the woodwork in the buffet was in bird's eye maple. The auditorium, devoid of the elaborate carvings, plaster work and decoration associated with the picture palaces of a by-gone age, was nevertheless memorable for several reasons. The expanse of side walls was broken by a series of plain pilasters, whilst across the ceiling were six fibrous plaster trough sound-breakers stepped down towards the proscenium to conceal the main house lighting which was supplemented by ceiling-mounted glass fittings adjacent to the small stage, itself equipped with two colour footlights. The seating capacity of the single storey auditorium was 930, the extra capacity having been achieved by utilisation of the stage area of the former theatre. The auditorium was tastefully decorated in pale pink to harmonise with the soft furnishings chosen personally by the proprietor's wife; the seating being in blue crushed velvet whilst the stage curtains were in dark blue with silver relief.

Much was made of the latest Western Electric sound equipment which had been installed. It was claimed that the Phoenix was the first cinema in the UK with this equipment and since it was not generally available on the market at that time, details were kept hush-hush. The provision of 'cry rooms' at the rear of the building was also most unique and attracted the attention of the national press. These two sound-proof rooms, equipped with their own glass windows and loud speaker system which was linked to the main theatre sound system, were incorporated to enable mothers with small children to watch the film without the noise of chatter and cries from their offspring proving troublesome to the remainder of the audiences. After a few years this novelty was dispensed with and the rooms became an integral part of the main auditorium by removal of the partition walls and the large windows therein. The resulting cosy alcoves at the rear of the auditorium provided a more permanent attraction for courting couples!

In July 1953, The Phoenix became the first picture house in Wallasey to be fitted with a wide screen, said to be 'twice bigger than normal wide screens'. The Phoenix became one of Wallasey's most popular cinemas of the time and despite the introduction of television, it continued to enjoy relatively good business during a period when box-office takings at many other picture houses in the region were depressed and many cinemas were being forced to close down. Eventually, however, Mr. Blond sold his cinema in the mid 1970's to the Hutchinson Group who sub-divided the auditorium soon after and converted the premises into two small 250 seater cinemas and provided a new entrance to the front section for bingo patrons. Bingo however, was not a success at the Phoenix, and this section was closed after only a few years operation. Films, on the other hand, continued to be profitable up until the early 1980's when, despite reduced entrance fees of £1 per seat and 60p for children on every night of the week, audience figures dwindled to such a low level that the Phoenix was no longer a viable operation and closure was inevitable. In 1983 Mr. G. Mander, manager of the Phoenix for thirteen years, attributed the demise of the cinema to the lack of suitable films. Whatever the true cause, the final programmes were shown on the 6th July 1983; *Tootsie* in Cine 1 and *An Officer and a Gentleman* in Cine 2. The cinema then lay empty for some years and was eventually demolished in 1988.

Palace Theatre
(Gaiety)

The amusement complex housing a grand hall, small concert hall, skating rink aquarium and aviary opened in New Brighton in the early 1880's. The main entrance was in Virginia Road, with additional access from New Brighton Promenade. The theatre became known as The Palace and Pavilion Theatre in 1893 and two years later it came under the control of the New Brighton Palace Company Ltd., with Mr. M. D. Ellery as Managing Director. The progress of the enterprise was steady until the arrival of the Tower, a few yards along the promenade, when the fortunes of the Palace began to decline. Plans were developed to revitalise the Palace and thus enable it to compete with the mighty Tower. To this end, a Manchester concern proposed erecting the biggest revolving wheel the world had ever seen with forty two carriages each holding forty passengers. However, the project was abandoned.

Next influence on the Palace was animated pictures and the theatre soon exploited these by becoming the second in Wallasey to be used as a cinema. Thus in 1906 when the premises became controlled by Wallasey Corportion, with Messrs. Lievers and Bennet the new lessees and Mr. Percy Penny the new manager, motion pictures by the Northern Cinematograph Trading Company were soon included in the mixed programme.

Palace Theatre (1906)

The first film programme comprised *The Great Thaw Trial* — the topic of the day; hundreds of side splitting comic pictures *My Word, if you're not off* — the popular saying illustrated; *The Limerick Craze* — showing how Jones did not win £5,000; *The Model Husband* — a real side splitter, no wife should be without him; *The Gamekeepers Dog* — man's faithful friend in time of trouble; and *The Hit of the Season* — shots of His Majesty King Edward VII and all the Royal family aboard the battleship Dreadnought. Other early films included *The Fisher Girls Wooing, Satan at Play* and *The Mill Girl* (a touching tale of factory life). The films were considered to be of good technical quality and of such a moral and refined nature that ladies, gentlemen and children would find them pleasing. Performances were each evening at 8.00 p.m. with a Grand Illuminated Childrens' Matinee on Saturday afternoons at 3.00 p.m. Admission cost between 2d and 1/6 for the evening house and 2d and 3d for the childrens' afternoon sessions.

The accommodation at the Palace however, was spartan, with its corrugated iron roof, poor heating and uncomfortable wooden bench seats on a flat ground floor. These seats had a tendency to deposit their occupants on the floor were those at one end suddenly to rise. The original seating capacity was 750 which was later expanded by the addition of a balcony. One entered the cinema through a small square vestibule that was on a level with the balcony and contained the paybox. The staircase leading to the ground floor was to the right hand side of the vestibule. The auditorium itself had plain walls with a deep painted dado and a high stage. The main decorative scheme was in off-white and

83

crimson with two plaster statues of Greek godesses in arched alcoves at either side of the stage. The Palace stage did not boast a fly tower, but back cloths on rollers were used for stage performances through from 1907 and these usually consisted of 'Go As You Please' talent contests. One feature remembered by a former patron was the male attendant who carried a stick that was applied across the backs of youngsters in the audience who created a disturbance during the performance.

Live shows became the main feature again in 1910, a trend which was continued by Mr. F. Vaughan when he became manager. Control changed hands yet again for a while when the Tivoli Company Ltd., acquired the premises but problems encountered with the construction of the Tivoli resulted in the Company selling the lease of the Palace to Mr. Ludwig Blattner (formerly with the Irving Theatre in Wallasey). He undertook major changes in order to create a new image for the theatre to enable it to compete with the more modern cinemas in the area. After a short period of closure for redecoration the premises re-opened as the Gaiety on Easter Monday 1914. The press proclaimed that the theatre had been splendidly decorated and improved beyond recognition. Modifications included an increased seating capacity to 1200 and the establishment of the Royal Bohemian Orchestra with Herr Heinrich Fieler and his violin. The orchestra, it was claimed, had been enthusiastically praised by Royalty on their recent visit to Liverpool.

Unfortunately, Blattner's reign at the Gaiety came to an abrupt end with the outbreak of war later in the year when he was forced to take up residence in an internment camp for the duration. (After the war, Ludwig Blattner was to become a film producer in London and also became well known as the inventor of a magnetic wire recorder known as the Blattnerphone.)

In October 1914, the Gaiety was advertising "numerous improvements — including modern heating apparatus installed throughout the building" and claimed to be "the cosiest entertainment in the district". It was further stressed that the theatre "is now worked by an all-British staff" under the management of Alfred Delmonte who later became musical director at the Marina. By December that year there was another change in administration and "beautiful pictures in conjunction with high-class orchestral music" were advertised with 'Go-as-you-please' contests every Friday, the profits from the first week being donated to the Wallasey War Relief Fund.

As the war progressed, Wednesday afternoon concerts for wounded soldiers became a regular feature at the Gaiety, with artistes giving their services free of charge. For a period during the winter season, the theatre was open for film performances on Mondays and Saturdays only. In 1916 a major fire swept through the complex destroying the skating rink and other parts of the building, but the theatre itself was saved as a result of the strenuous efforts by the firemen. For a while the theatre was known as the Palace Picture Playhouse. After the war in 1920, the lease was taken over by the well-known fairground operator Pat Collins Jnr. and the theatre then became known as Collins' Palace Cinema. Films were continued as the main entertainment, but for a time during 1923 there was a reversion to purely live shows when "The highest-class concert parties in the country" were advertised. Throughout 1924 and 1925 the theatre remained closed but re-opened on Whit Monday 1926 with Joseph W. Gabriel (a well-known local pianist and conductor) as lessee and Reginald Eysenck (formerly of the Lyceum Picture House, Eastbourne) as manager.

The theatre was advertised as redecorated and re-seated and even by this time prices were still in the range of 3d to 1/3. Performances included daily matinees at 2.30 p.m. and evening shows continuous from 6.15 to 10.15 p.m. The opening programme was *The Sky Rider* featuring Captain Nungesser and Gladys Walton with a Larry Semon Comedy, *Frauds and Frenzies*, *Pathe Pictorial* and *Pathe Gazette*, plus a musical interlude by Joseph Gabriel and his orchestra.

The Palace finally closed on December 11th 1926, with a showing of *Spook Ranch* featuring Hoot Gibson. Plans to develop the site were mooted in 1932 and after standing derelict for several years, the Palace was eventually demolished in 1933 to make way for the construction of The New Palace Amusement Park.

Pictureland

In November 1912, a certain H. Phillips applied for permission to use the ground floor of Egerton Hall, a small public hall at the corner of Egerton Street and Mason Street, New Brighton, for exhibiting animated pictures.

Double entrance doors at the corner of the two storey building in Mason Street opened into a small vestibule and at the top of a short flight of steps was the paybox, to the right of which was the entrance into the flat-floored auditorium with seating for 200. The exit doors opened out on the right hand side of the hall into Mason Street and the small projection room was adjacent to the pay-box.

The facilities provided were extremely basic, and opening and closing dates are not known, but, it appears that the hall was only used for less than a year for showing films, after which time it reverted to its former use.

Queen's Picture House

The Queen's in Poulton Road was Wallasey's first purpose built cinema. It was opened on the 4th November 1911, with a programme of films on subjects ranging from drama, comedy, travel, education and news. Under the management of Mr. E.F. Evans admission was at 3d, 4d, 6d and 9d and three-hour shows ran from 7.00 p.m. during the week with matinees at 3.00 p.m. on Wednesdays. On Saturdays, the programme was continuous between 6.00 and 10.30 p.m.

The building immodestly claimed to be the finest Picturedrome in the North of England. The exterior design of the building was particularly attractive with a curved glass verandah encircling the frontage, and the roof was topped with a magnificent dome. The white fibrous plaster covering the brickwork produced a dazzling effect which, at night, was further enhanced by some 350 electric light bulbs.

To ensure the comfort of the audience, no expense had been spared on the interior decor as exemplified by the lushly carpeted marble entrance, the gilt decorations and the crimson plush upholstery on the 800 tip-up seats with

Queens Picture House (1948)

matching thick crimson carpeting in the main hall. The hall itself was said to be lofty and cool. It was spacious and the seats were arranged on a sloping floor raked to a height of six feet at the rear. This ensured that from every seat there was a good view of the screen, which was painted on the back wall and surrounded by an arched fibrous plaster frame; there was no balcony. Three huge fans cooled the building during summer, whilst a modern heating system provided warmth in the cooler months. Concern over audience safety is illustrated by the fire-proof design of the hall, coupled with the provision of an above average number of emergency exits. The reliability of performances was guaranteed by use of two of the best available bioscopes in the operating room and the employment of competent staff. An orchestra provided music both to accompany the silent movies as well as providing interludes between films.

Until the talkies arrived at the beginning of the thirties, the Queen's remained substantially unaltered despite rumours in 1927 that extensive construction work had been scheduled to build a balcony and to enlarge the premises by extending the frontage. The management did, however, change when Mr. R. P. Rutherford took over and the Paramount Orchestra was employed to provide musical entertainment under the baton of Mr. H. Watkinson. (Mr. Rutherford was also to be in charge of four other halls owned by Wirral Picturedrome Ltd., and was for many years a leading figure in the North Western Branch of the Cinema Exhibitors Association.)

With the advent of the talkie era, modifications were necessary. Thus a new screen on the stage platform was needed to accommodate the sound reproduction equipment. This also resulted in a new proscenium, new royal blue velour drapes and rather unusually, globular light fittings on tripod stands, one either side of the screen. The first talkie presentation *Smiling Irish Eyes* featuring Coleen Moore, was screened on the 12th May 1930, together with an all-talkie comedy called *Beach Babes*.

From the 30th November 1934, Friday night entertainment at the Queen's included variety on stage and the return of the Blue Ribbon Orchestra, which had previously been dispensed with at the end of the silent era. This arrangement continued until the end of the year. The Queen's was a small and intimate cinema, resisting temptations to mimic the neon light and chromium trappings of the newer and larger palaces. Even so, it retained a regular following during the post-war period right up to the mid 1950's, when even the introduction of CinemaScope failed to bolster box office takings at a time of rapidly diminishing audiences. The cinema closed its doors on the 18th July, 1959 with Frankie Vaughan in *Lady is a Square* and *Gun Battle in Monterey*. This was the seventh cinema in the area to close and the fourth to close in Wallasey that year. The Queen's Picture House Circuit was founded by Mr. C. Collins, a local man and although they had also closed the Queen's in Liverpool, establishments in Wigan, Warrington and Waterloo were still operating at the time. Since the closure of the Queen's, the building has been used as a car show room and a supermarket.

Artist impression of Queens prior to construction

The old Queen's Cinema, in Poulton Road, photographed in the late 1940's.

Royal

The premises at 94/96 King Street, Egremont, which had been used as a drill hall and skating rink, were converted by Wallasey Cinemas Ltd., (with Mr. W.D. Burrows as Managing Director) into a 850 seater Cinedrome which opened on the 4th November, 1912. At the time it was hailed to be the largest picture palace in the district. Performances were continuous from 6.30 to 10.45 p.m. with 2.30 p.m. matinees on Saturdays. Admission charges in those days were 2d, 3d and 6d.

The simple white-painted facade was relieved by half timbering and two sets of leaded light windows between which was an illuminated glass sign displaying the name of the house. Two pairs of Georgian glass panelled doors led from the street to the small foyer with its central pay box. The plain, wide auditorium contained a steeply raked floor to provide a good view of the screen from all seats; the absence of a balcony aided the ventilation of the building thereby improving the quality of the atmosphere. The installation of the best projection equipment ensured that pictures were both steady and clear.

The opening programme, which resulted in a full house, consisted of six films, namely *The Wheel of Destruction* (a drama said to contain one of the most vivid portrayals of a motor car accident ever witnessed), *The Church Round The Corner*, *Jenkin's Hydraulics*, *Wanted – A Divorce*, *Red Ruby's Redemption*, and the Western drama, *In Swift Waters*. In addition patrons were invited to "come and hear the Cinfonium", described as a cinema-vocal combination and advertised as "One of the music marvels of the age and well worth repeated visits".

The history of the Royal can be considered one of innovation. The first unique venture was the introduction of serials in 1913 when, on the 20th January, it was announced that *Our Navy* a serial film in eight instalments, would be shown over a period of four weeks. On Wednesday the 26th June 1929, the Royal also became the first cinema in Wallasey to show talking pictures. The first

Royal (1920's)

Royal (1954)

programme featured a one-reeler of J.H. Squire's _Celeste Octet_ of which it was said that the intonation was as clear and as fresh as though the orchestra itself was on the stage. A sketch from Dickens' _Bleak House_ with the famous actor Bransby Williams was also included in the programme together with the London Ceremony of the Trooping of the Colour. Interestingly, however, the feature film was still silent and for several weeks the Royal Orchestra was retained to provide accompaniment for these mixed programmes of silent and talkie presentations. The use of all-British sound and talkie apparatus was emphasized.

The next major modifications to the cinema occurred in 1931 with the construction of a new verandah and then on the 24th February 1934, with the installation of upgraded British Talking Pictures sound equipment at enormous expense. The new apparatus gave extended frequency range to enhance the quality of speech and music in terms of tone and apparent power output; "The talk of London can now be heard for the first time in Cheshire at this theatre only" it was claimed. Following the suicide of the manager, Mr. Alfred Brewer, in September 1935, former chief projectionist Hector McQueen took over and recalls that he was responsible for the installation of the first set of draw curtains to be used at the Royal, these being made up by his wife in striking rainbow-coloured material. Mr. McQueen also remembers at this time, a triangular platform at the left hand side of the screen which could be used when there was a live performer in attendance, such as a pianist or singer.

In September 1936, David Forrester, Theatres Manager of Manchester, took over ownership and the Royal closed for a week for refurbishment. The cinema underwent a complete redecoration and new seats, curtains and lighting were

Royal (1960's) (after closure)

installed; a feature of the house when it re-opened on the 21st September, was the blending of warm colours coupled with the Wedgewood-like effect of the sculptured figures which had been made to stand out in pleasing relief from the background of gradually diminishing sun colours. The picture house was then claimed to be one of the smartest cinemas in the country. Another novelty of the 1936 modernisations, was the announcement by Mr. McQueen, that Rediffusion sound equipment had been installed to enable BBC radio programmes to be played to the cinema audience for half an hour prior to the commencement of film shows.

From the 24th October 1937, special Sunday concerts were introduced for the winter season, the first being with Jack Leigh and his original Embassey Band and fifteen talented performers, including violinist Patrizov, formerly of the Capitol. Yet another innovation at the Royal was the introduction by another manager, A.E. Drennen, of Slidograph competitions in September 1938. Patrons were invited to submit snapshot negatives to be shown on the screen for an entry fee of 6d per photograph, which covered the cost of slide preparation; prizes of £5, £3 and £2 were awarded to the winners. 'Gift Nights', a somewhat frivolous novelty, was introduced on Tuesdays and Fridays for a short while at the Royal in January 1939. To chose a winner, an attendant stood on the stage and, as music played, he manipulated a mirror to reflect the light from the film projector into the darkened auditorium. When the music ceased the person on whom the light rested was invited up on to the stage to receive a free gift. Twelve prizes in all were awarded, ranging from towels to table-cloths, and sausages to cwts. of coal. The manager also offered a special gift of lipstick to the lady who would kiss him on stage, and as a finale, two packages of black puddings were thrown to people in the front stalls. It would appear, however, that the licensing authority did not take kindly to such 'goings on' at a Wallasey cinema and the management at the Royal were forced to seek other means of attracting custom.

Other changes resulted from the purchase of the premises in 1948 by Messrs. Whilma Wilkie and Henry Neck, proprietors of the New Brighton Palace amusement complex. Following closure of the theatre on the 16th August for four months, the interior was completely gutted and the Royal upgraded at a cost of £10,000; £7-8,000 being devoted to the premises which included renewing the ceiling, floor, carpet, heating, seats (with an expanded seating capacity of 872), and screen. The latter was capable of being moved to the back of the stage to permit live performances, a facility that was taken advantage of on the re-opening night only. A further £2,500 was devoted to installation of the latest G.B. Kalee projectors and sound equipment. Mr. T. Foster was appointed manager and licensee. The cinema re-opened on the 13th December with Bob Hope, Bing Crosby and Dorothy Lamour in *Road to Rio.*

Yet another innovation came at the end of 1954, when the Royal became the only cinema in Wallasey with stereophonic sound. New French festoon-style silver satin curtains were also installed, together with an ultra-wide 30ft Cinema-Scope screen which necessitated the dismantling of the proscenium. The first CinemaScope film was *The Robe* which was screened on Monday the 6th December 1954. After closure in 1958 for a while the Royal re-opened in November of that year, with Mr. G.A. Taylor as Director (previously manager of the Liscard Picture Palace). Tactics used to attract audiences were reduced admission charges and a wider variety of films. However, the battle against declining audiences was finally lost in January 1967, when the then proprietor, Mr. Albert Johnson, was forced to close the Royal for good as a cinema. The final programme was the 'double horror' bill *The Day of the Triffids* and *King Kong vs Godzilla.* This was the eighth cinema to close in eleven years in the town. Mr. T. Foster, who had been manager of the Royal for the last eighteen years, moved to The Court in New Brighton, one of the few remaining cinemas open in Wallasey at the time; the others being the ABC Liscard, The Gaumont in Egremont, and the Phoenix in Wallasey Village.

The outside of the building has changed little during its life-time and since its closure it has been used as a bingo hall and more recently as a snooker club.

Royal as a Snooker Hall (1989)

Tivoli

The Tivoli was situated on the promenade close to the New Brighton pier and the frontage included six shops and a cafe above, which extended along the whole width of the building. The auditorium was quite ornate with a balcony that curved round almost to the boxes at either side of the stage. Sight lines were good from all parts of the house and there was a well equipped stage complete with fly tower.

This 636 seat theatre opened on 6th April 1914, with a variety show that had Lilly Langtry at the top of the bill. The theatre was originally under the management of F.V.Ross, but in September 1921 was bought by Pat Collins for £37,500 and eventually was sold at a loss in October 1928 for £27,000 to Provincial Cinematograph Theatres. Throughout its six decades in operation the theatre was rarely used as a cinema, even though an edition of the Pathe Gazette newsreel was shown to complete most variety bills prior to the introduction of the talkies. The reason is clear: between the time of its opening and 1923 the Tivoli was the greatest Vaudeville success on Merseyside as indicated by the subsequent acquisition of the Kings Theatre, Seacombe, for £8,000 from the profits from the Tivoli.

It was in 1923 that the theatre was first used as the Tivoli Super Cinema, opening on Monday 19th February with *Saturday Night*, a Paramount Super Play Cecil B. De Mille production, starring Leatrice Joy and Conrad Nagel, supported by *A Sporting Double* and the super serial *Across Two Continents*. The Piccadilly Orchestra played "special musical settings" and "magnificent colour schemes", and "clear pictures" were also advertised, the prices being 4d, 6d and 1/-. However, from April 2nd there was a reversion to stage revues and F.V. Ross was again managing the theatre at the end of 1925.

Tivoli (circa 1920)

GRAND   **TIVOLI,**   NEW
RE-OPENING.   BRIGHTON.
MONDAY NEXT, JUNE 9th.——FOR SIX DAYS—
———————— ENORMOUS ATTRACTION ! ————————
JACK HOLT, LILA LEE, RALPH GRAVES,
in the 100% TALKING AIR DRAMA—
" FLIGHT."

Matinees Daily—at 2·30 p.m.   CIRCLE 1/-. STALLS 8d. PIT 4d.
Evenings—Continuous—from 8·15 p.m. CIRCLE 1/3. STALLS 8d. PIT 8d.

TALKIES AT THE TIVOLI.

It was announced in October 1928 that the future policy of the new owners would be to present 'the best and latest of pictures in turn with first class plays and musical comedies'. Their first film presentation was on Monday the 8th October with *Ramona* starring Dolores del Rio, plus *Woman's Wares*, and non-stop programmes were advertised from 2.30 to 10.30 p.m. with prices from 6d to 1/3d. The projection installation was reported to be one of the very best of its kind and a special screen had been fixed "to enable everyone all over the house to have a clear, uninterrupted and undistorted view of the film". The Tivoli Orchestra under the direction of Richard Tomlinson provided musical interludes. Films continued to alternate with stage programmes up till 6th April 1929, when after a period of closure, the Tivoli resumed purely stage entertainment from the 1st of July 1929.

Tivoli Super Cinema.

Moving with the spirit of the times, Mr. Pat Collins, junr.. has converted the Tivoli, New Brighton, into a super cinema. If one may judge of the hearty reception accorded the change by good houses on Monday night, everything augers well for the success of the enterprise. Nothing more beautiful could be imagined than the clearness of the animated pictures projected on the screen, which gave huge delight to the audiences. The "Piccadilly" orchestra played appropriate music with excellent taste and judgment.

To-night (Saturday) will be shown Priscilla Dean in "Reputation," supported by the great masterpiece, "A Wonderful Story," a drama of intense human interest. There will be a matinee to-day at 3 o'clock.

The next and last film season at the Tivoli came in 1930 when a Grand reopening with 'Talkies at the Tivoli' was announced from 19th June with Western Electric Sound System installed. The film was *Flight* with Jack Holt and Lila Lee, and prices were circle 1/3, stalls 9d, pit 6d, with matinees at 2.30 p.m. and evenings continuous from 6.15 p.m. Only five weeks later on 14th July, the opening of the variety season was announced, and from this time henceforth films were not to be seen again at the Tivoli. The theatre survived more changes of management and several periods of closure. Thus, for a few months in 1937, the theatre was known as the New Tivoli but the title was soon dropped. The premises remained closed between 1939 and 1940, when they re-opened only to be closed again a few months later as a result of war damage. It was not until 1945 that the Tivoli was re-opened by Leam Production Ltd., once again primarily as a theatre. However, in common with other provincial theatres and music halls, efforts to save it from closure in the early to mid 1950's were to no avail and its end as a theatre finally came in April 1955. After this, the stalls area was used for a short time as an amusement arcade and final demolition came after fire damage in 1976.

Demolition of Tivoli Theatre
(January 1978)

Tower Theatre

The history of this building is a somewhat sad affair. Without a doubt this was the most imposing building in Wirral and arguably the statistics make it one of the most unusual theatres in the country at the time. The Tower was built on the river front in New Brighton between 1896 and 1897 as an entertainment complex overlooking the River Mersey. The extensive grounds housed gardens, a fairground and zoo. The main huge building carried a 500ft high tower, and, with a total height of 620 ft above sea level, it was higher than the 520 ft Blackpool Tower built in 1895. Indeed the Tower at New Brighton was described as 'the highest structure in the United Kingdom' and its construction cost the lives of at least six men. There were four lifts, and trips to the top of the tower cost 6d. The building itself comprised a ballroom below which was a theatre with a seating capacity in excess of 3,000 proving to be the largest theatre in the Provinces. The depth of the stage, which was claimed to be the largest in the world, amounted to 72 ft and the proscenium was 45 ft wide. The auditorium was of amphitheatre design.

Over the years the theatre was used for a range of entertainment purposes, mainly on a seasonal basis, but with orchestral concerts (eg with Elgar appearing in person) and musical reviews at the forefront. As early as 1904 the latest Animated Pictures by the Royal Bioscope were advertised including shots of the Russo-Japanese War. In 1907, stage shows were accompanied by "The Truly Wonderful Chronophone Talking, Singing and Dancing Pictures".

NEW BRIGHTON TOWER   1897 - 1919

Tower Theatre 'Victory Concert' (1945)

Tower on fire (1969)

As a result of neglect, the elements took their toll on the steel tower which deteriorated so badly as a result of the lack of maintenance, that it had to be demolished over a two year period in 1918-1920. This, however, did not affect the remainder of the complex which continued to function as normal.

Use of the theatre itself continued to oscillate between live entertainment and films. In 1925 Gracie Fields appeared at the Tower Theatre in *By Request*, a review written and produced by Archie Pitt. Interestingly, during rehearsals Mr. Pitt made a film of Miss Fields teaching the cast to dance the Charleston in the grounds. This film was then shown as *A Review in the Making* at the Tower and other cinemas throughout the county soon after.

In 1926 'Variety Artists and Pictures' were advertised nightly, whilst two big stage attractions for Easter 1927 were Jack Hylton's Famous Band on Good Friday, and Dame Clara Butt and Party on Easter Sunday. These were complemented by cinema performances from 3.00 to 10.30 p.m., except on Good Friday. For a period during the 1920's the enormous stage was also used to accommodate two badminton courts. A former Wallasey resident, Mrs. Betty Anderson, recalled watching the film show in the theatre while waiting to play badminton, the films being projected onto the safety curtain at the front of the stage, thus leaving the stage itself free for the badminton players. She also remembers how cold and draughty the theatre was and how poorly supported were the picture shows. It is perhaps not surprising therefore, to find that from 1928 films were no longer on the programme and its main use was to stage wrestling matches and occasional concerts. A revival occurred in 1954 when, from May 29th, a summer season of comedy films and a puppet theatre were advertised on Saturdays and Sunday continuously between 2.00 and 6.00 p.m., at a cost of 6d. This continued up to the 22nd August and thereafter films were discontinued and the condition of the building deteriorated rapidly after a period of disuse, only to become so badly destroyed by a spectacular fire on the 5th April 1969, that the charred shell had to be demolished.

The Trocadero

Trocadero – Manager Robin Jones and staff (1935)

A company was formed in 1919 to acquire a block of lock-up shops and the Albert Billiard Hall, Victoria Road, (the main thoroughfare of Wallasey's seaside resort of New Brighton) with the aim of converting the premises into a picture house. The managing director of the new enterprise was Mr. George Temperley, previously manager of the Liscard Palace and newly demobilised from the Army. The architects were Messrs. Wright and Hamlyn of Warrington. After an initial difficulty in gaining access to the billiard hall and a court battle to evict the original owners, the project was completed in 1922 by the builders, Messrs. George Snape and Son of Birkenhead.

The cinema was built from reinforced concrete and was of fire-proof construction. The main frontage was executed in cream tinted terra cotta and the central portion, which rose above the entrance, was finished with a heavy pedimented gable and well proportioned windows. Either side were lock-up shops surmounted by a plain parapet. Throughout the length of the frontage in Victoria Road, was a wrought-iron and glass verandah to provide shelter in bad weather for patrons queuing outside.

Inside, the cinema was capable of accommodating some 900 people in what was considered at that time, to be most luxurious surroundings. The main entrance from Victoria Road, with its marble paving provided access through pairs of handsome mahogany swing doors to a spacious hall panelled in keeping with the entrance doors, and with a deeply coffered ceiling to produce a rich and chaste effect preparing the way for the further decorative schemes of which it was the forerunner. Leading directly from the hall were the entrance doors to the auditorium and immediately to the left was an elaborate staircase, with its massive balustrade. The stairs led to the foyer on the first floor, which in turn gave access to the luxurious balcony which had been constructed on a slope so as to ensure every seat had a clear view of the screen.

Trocadero (circa 1946)

The inside walls were of simple and restrained style. The main piers were run up as pilasters finished with enriched brackets from which sprung arched ribs of decorative plasterwork across the ceiling. The intervening wall spaces between the pilasters were richly panelled in modelled plaster work leading up to an effective treatment over the circular windows, and surmounted at the eaves by a well-proportioned classic cornice. The infilling to the ceiling was also effectively broken up by a series of panels and enriched ventilating gratings. The proscenium front and arch was boldly treated forming a fitting frame to the silver screen and its draperies. The tip-up seats were upholstered in blue corduroy velveteen and finished with mahogany backs and arms.

The heating was provided by a low-pressure hot-water system, whilst the air conditioning comprised a blower fan to provide fresh, warm air at a low level to eliminate floor draughts and as a supply of make-up air to replace the 'vitiated and smoke-laden atmosphere' removed via the ventilation gratings in the ceiling. The premises were also equipped with electric vacuum cleaning apparatus. The emergency electricity supply was from a petrol-driven generator, while the main lighting was of an 'indirect' type with handsomely-cut alabaster bowls and metalwork in keeping with the general decorative scheme. Much was made of the adequacy of the electric cabling, metal switch boxes, fuses, switchboards etc., which were of the latest Home Office pattern. Numerous emergency exits were easily accessible from all parts of the house. The projection room was entirely cut off from the public space and access was only via an outside door, thus ensuring immunity from risk of fire from the main building.

The "Last Word in Picture Houses" was formally opened by the Mayor of Wallasey, Alderman A. Quinn, on the 1st of June 1922. The lead film was William Farnum in *Perjury*, which was followed by a selection of comedies, news items and educational topics such as *The Gaumont Graphic, Around the Town, Horses to Follow, Would Be Suicide* and *Aesop's Fables*. Music was provided by the Trocadero Symphony Orchestra under the baton of Mr. Bescoby. The acting manager was Mr. C.H. Hankinson, who had previous experience with the Hippodrome and the Tivoli Theatre. Admission charges were 6d, 9d and 1/3.

Although the construction had been financed by local businessmen, the Trocadero changed hands soon after opening to the Liverpool based First Federated Cinemas (J.F. Wood circuit). Then in 1928 it became part of the rapidly expanding Gaumont-British circuit under whose control it remained until closure, the manager for many years being Robin Jones. The first talkie film to be shown was the appropriately named *The Great Gabbo* with Erich von Stroheim on Monday the 24th of March 1930.

In November 1936, the circle was reconstructed, re-seated and redecorated, the old alabaster light fittings being replaced by V-shaped metal framed pendant fittings, with amber tinted glass. When war broke out in September 1939, the glass was removed from these fittings to avoid the possibility of it being showered onto the audience during the course of an air raid. Later on the fittings themselves were removed and replaced by a single large amber-coloured lamp in each instance. Along the front edge of the stage, facing the audience, were sections of red frosted glass, illuminated from behind by the footlights, and another wartime innovation was the replacement of the centre section of glass by an oblong box with opaque glass and two panels, one in red — designed to light up and indicate to the audience that the air raid 'Alert' had sounded, and the other in green — to indicate when it was 'All Clear'. At this time the curtains were royal blue with gold trim and matching pelmet.

One problem at 'The Troc' was the height of the screen on the very shallow stage platform, which resulted in occupants of the first few rows in the stalls having a very distorted view of the image on the screen. Installation of CinemaScope in May 1955 gave a picture only slightly wider than the original screen, but on the 22nd September 1956, the Trocadero was closed with only a few days' warning, the news being announced while redecoration and provision of a new canopy replacing the old glass verandah was still in progress. The building now serves as a supermarket.

Vienna Hall

In August 1907 a working mens' hall on the corner of Brighton Street and Vienna Street, Seacombe, operated by one A.B. Kopetzky, became a full-time cinema, advertising the Royal American Bioscope. This building had originally been a furniture store and was to continue to show films together with variety turns until 1914.

The first advertisement claimed that 30,000 pictures were shown at every performance (referring to the number of picture frames passing through the hand-cranked projector), and also advertised "Songs beautifully illustrated". Programmes were changed every week and were twice nightly at 7.00 and 9.00 p.m. with matinees every Saturday at 3.00 p.m. Admission was 2d, 4d and 6d, with children half-price.

In July 1914 it was announced that the Vienna Hall would shortly close prior to extensive alterations, and by the end of the month it had ceased operation. Demolition was shortly to commence to make way for a completely new cinema, the Marina.

Vienna Hall

Wallasey Picturedrome

The history of the cinema was short and of little significance. The 200 seater Wesleyan Chapel in Wallasey Village opened in 1885 and was vacated in 1910 when the congregation moved to alternative premises in Claremount Road. The building was converted into the Wallasey Picturedrome and began advertising films on the 6th of March 1911, under the management of Miss M. Hardy, with piano accompaniments by Mr. Clutterbuck. "Popular Pictures at Popular Prices" were advertised with performances at 6.30 and 8.30 p.m. daily and a Saturday matinee at 3.00 p.m. A feature of the opening performances was 'The Love of a Chrysanthemum', described as a very artistic coloured production. Admission was 2d, 4d and 6d in the tip-up seats.

The pianist was supplemented first by a singer, Miss M. Solari and then by a comedian, Mr. Hal Rowe. There were few subsequent programme advertisements. A change in management at the end of 1911 was announced when the cinema re-opened on Monday the 11th December, but two weeks later the Picturedrome was to close again for "alterations and cleaning". The re-opening came on Monday the 8th January with a star programme including a variety act known as The Two Kraks. The picture house ceased operation in early 1912 and the building, which was converted into shops, still stands as 131 to 137 Wallasey Village.

PICTUREDROME, VILLAGE RD WALLASEY

Winter Gardens

Messrs. A. Douglass and H.E. Jones leased the old Conservative Club in Atherton Street, New Brighton, for Saturday evening concerts in 1907. In February the following year the Alexandra Hall became the Winter Gardens with programmes of plays and films, complete with an orchestra and palms. Because of the cramped conditions, however, both on the stage and in the dressing rooms, a limited company was formed at the end of 1909 with the task of rebuilding the Winter Gardens. Within as little as five weeks in the middle of 1910 the old auditorium was removed to be replaced by a grand circle. Improved dressing rooms and an enlarged stage measuring 60 ft x 33 ft were provided, together with the wonder of the time — electric lighting. Throughout World War One, the Winter Gardens remained open and in 1919, Mr. Douglass became the sole owner.

The old Winter Gardens with 'house full' sign on display

The history of the building which stands at present on the site, however, dates to more recent times. In 1924 Mr. A.C. Douglass proposed rebuilding the theatre but the suggestion was rejected by his father. By 1929 all of the directors however, supported the proposal and in February 1931 work commenced on the project. It was thought that much of the original structure could be retained, but in the event, it became clear that the old Winter Gardens, with the exception of the dressing rooms, needed to be demolished and a new theatre built in its place. This was achieved in a record four months and the new theatre opened on the 27th of June, 1931.

This large 1,400 seater building, designed by Messrs. T. Taliesin Rees and R. Holt, had a striking facade with canopy, display boards, six entrance doors and floodlights for night time illumination.

Inside the large entrance foyer were a box office, two pay booths and a ladies' cloak room; the gentlemen's cloak room was downstairs. Stairs either side of the hall led to a lounge with facilities for refreshments, including a bar. Above this mezzanine floor was a large balcony. An unusual feature of the balcony was the provision of two private boxes at either extremity of the circle front that curved outwards especially to accommodate them. Either side of the stage above each of the two exits there was an ornamental canopy supported by fibrous plaster columns. The main hall itself measured 87 ft 6 in x 57 ft 9 in. Beneath the balcony was a dome, illuminated by concealed lighting, whilst six groups of high-powered lights fitted with special reflectors in the ceiling void, provided the main illumination for the auditorium, the light passing through rectangular figured glass panels flush with the ceiling. The theatre boasted a large and well-equipped stage with fly-tower and generous dressing room facilities. Seats were of the tip-up variety with arm rests.

WINTER GARDENS, NEW BRIGHTON, ADJOINING RAILWAY STATION ENTRANCE

Winter Gardens (1931)

Winter Gardens (1931)

Winter Gardens (1931)

The Winter Gardens had a rather schizophrenic existence as indicated by a constant shift between use for live performances and film shows; its heart however, appeared to be in stage productions. From the time it was built it was clear that its destiny was uncertain. It was designed primarily as a theatre but with a projection room built on as an insurance. After a promising start within its first year of operation, which relied on live performances, the theatre was already in trouble and the takings slumped to £47 in one week. The management appealed for support and reduced entrance charges; after a period of once-a-month closures the business survived, but stage productions continued until the mid 1930's.

In 1936, the Winter Gardens was taken over by Cheshire Picture Halls (later to become S.M. Super Cinemas), even though Mr. Douglass remained as managing director. The new owners installed the most up to date projection apparatus with Western Electric Wide Range Sound System, and a "short cinema season" was announced from Monday the 4th of May, commencing with *The Passing of the Third Floor Back* starring Conrad Veidt. However, within two weeks the cinema closed on the 16th of May for extensive modernisation which included some changes to the internal appearance including remodelling of the proscenium surround and treatment of the walls and ceiling with plastic paint. The two balcony boxes were removed and the decorative plaster work above the exits flanking the stage were replaced by modern plaster work with concealed lighting illuminating coved semi-circular panels which were sprayed with gold paint. The general colour scheme consisted of warm oatmeal coloured walls with green and gold bands with black and green dados, the proscenium area being finished in green, gold and tangerine, while the ceiling was coloured a light green with a silver clouded effect over the balcony and ventilation grilles. The cafe-lounge had also been completely re-constructed with new furniture and new concealed lighting. Other improvements included new seats in the circle, rubberised coverings for staircases, passages and lounge and also installation of an electric emergency lighting system to replace the original gas version.

On re-opening on the 1st of June 1936 it became customary for patrons to wear smart evening dress. Stage productions were most prominent through the summer season until the 5th of October, when a further short season of films was introduced until the 4th of January the following year. Live performances again dominated the programme for the next few years, during which time the projection equipment was transferred to the newly-opened Regal Cinema in Birkenhead.

At the back end of 1939, the government ordered all places of entertainment to close. Despite the order being revoked, from September the 15th of that year the Winter Gardens remained closed, during which time new Kalee 11 film projectors, an RCA High Fidelity sound System, and a new cinema screen were installed, together with the Compton 'Theatrone' electric organ which had been transferred from the Regal, Birkenhead. The main speakers for the organ were placed above the exits flanking the stage and enclosures were specially constructed to harmonise with the existing plasterwork. Further speakers were housed beneath the stage. The Winter Gardens remained closed until the 26th of December 1939, when a special Christmas production of *Alice in Wonderland*, with Donald Wolfit was staged. On the 1st of January 1940, the theatre, thereafter known as the New Winter Gardens, under the auspices of S.M. Super Cinemas Ltd., was given a grand opening with Alan Lusty at the Organ and a showing of *Captain Fury* starring Brian Aherne and Victor McLagen. The attractive cream and gold organ console was placed on the stage behind the screen against a background of black velour curtains that would be opened to reveal a backcloth onto which slides could be projected. In order to facilitate an immediate changeover from films to organ interlude, the screen curtain track and motor were attached to the counterweighted screen frame, together with the talkie speakers and these could all be 'flown' within less than a minute. Unfortunately, soon afterwards both the organist and the new manager, Mr. J.J. Lambert (previously with the New Ferry Lyceum) received their call-up papers for the war effort. Mrs. Crompton, the chief cashier, replaced the manager but no organist was provided.

During the war Wallasey suffered badly from the German air raids that commenced in May 1940 and one bomb that narrowly missed the stage end of the Winter Gardens, demolished the old dressing room block that had been part of the original theatre but fortunately the main cinema building escaped serious damage. However, the film to be screened the following day was destroyed, making it necessary to use the standby feature *Naughty Marietta* starring Jeanette MacDonald.

Winter Gardens (1936)

Winter Gardens (1936)

Winter Gardens (1938)

Because of the war, the attendances at the Winter Gardens had dwindled and at the beginning of 1941 it again closed until the Whitsuntide of 1942. In April that year a horse-drawn wagon was to be seen on the streets bearing large poster boards advertising "Grand Re-Opening of the Winter Gardens on Whit Monday". The opening attraction was the Abbott and Costello film *Hold that Ghost* with the famous BBC broadcasting and recording star Mr. Florence de Jong entertaining at the organ. After this performance the organ was little used until the appointment of Charles Massey as organist and manager in November 1942.

The following year live shows were again introduced into the programme, including the immensely popular Wednesday night talent spots, and these continued to provide full houses — an extremely uncommon occurrence at the Winter Gardens. The popularity of these amateur shows led to 'Guest Night' stage shows on Friday evenings, when winners of the talent contests and some professional artists would be engaged. These continued even when Mr. Massey moved to open his own cinema, the Court, and was replaced by Mr. John Wright as organist and manager.

The chief projectionist at this time was Cyril Bolton, formerly of the Kings, and he remembers a couple of accidents that occurred during the stage shows. The first took place towards the end of a show when one of the stage hands was hurrying along the 'cat walk' above the stage and accidentally knocked against a large drum filled with water designed for use in the event of an incendiary bomb falling on the stage. The impact caused the drum and its contents to crash down onto the stage below, missing the organist by inches, but giving him an unexpected drenching. Fortunately, the audience did not witness this mishap as the main curtain had been dropped a moment earlier.

The other incident came at a time when the motor that operated the screen curtains was temporarily out of action and it was necessary for one of the projectionists to go down to the stage before the commencement of the stage show to close the curtains, a task not made easier by the fact that the curtain controller was mounted on the screen frame about six feet from the stage floor. When the projectionist concerned failed to return to the box to man one of the two spotlights, Cyril Bolton went down to the stage to find out what was delaying him but was unable to see any trace of the missing fourth projectionist. However, just as he was about to return to the projection room, he heard a noise from above the stage and looked up to see the unfortunate man suspended thirty foot above the stage clinging to the side of the screen frame. Being a small man, he had found it necessary to stand on a chair to operate the curtains and had overbalanced when the screen was suddenly raised just before the curtains had completely closed. In order to save himself from falling, he had grabbed onto the screen frame and had been carried up with it into the fly tower above the stage. Even in a situation such as this, the show must go on, so it wasn't until the end of the act then in progress that the drop curtain was lowered and the screen returned to stage level with its unwilling passenger.

By the early 1950's stage shows had been dropped from the film programme, but the steep decline in audiences then affecting all cinemas led to S.M. Cinemas in 1954, renting the theatre to Nita Valerie and her Winter Garden Players to present a summer season of plays from June until November of that year. By the end of 1954, the S.M. Group had sold the Winter Gardens to the Essoldo Circuit who installed CinemaScope before re-opening the cinema on the 27th of December with a showing of *The Robe*. From the 21st of May 1956, Essoldo staged their own live shows, 'Essoldo Follies' with Eddie Molloy and Julie Dey plus Frank Gordon at the organ which had now been moved into the orchestra pit. The final reversion to films occurred in October 1956, but in January 1957, the Winter Gardens closed with the double feature programme *The Moonraker* starring George Baker and Sylvia Sims, plus John Ericson in *Oregon Passage*. The curtains closed for the last time to the tune of the march 'Old Comrades'. This was the last of New Brighton's four cinemas. Ironically, it was Mr. H. Monday's thirteenth unlucky week as manager of the Winter Gardens when the closure came; fourteen other staff were affected.

After opening in the mid 1960's as a Bingo Hall, the owners, Legalite Bingo, within a few years were bankrupt. The building, with its two offices, one store and a club area plus a modern, rear, two-storey extension housing eight bed sitting rooms, kitchen, bathroom, WC's and store were put to auction at a reserve price of £15,000 but there were no takers. At one stage the building was sold to a firm of wood merchants for use as a warehouse but planning permission was not forthcoming. To this day the building stands derelict.

Winter Gardens as Essoldo (circa 1960)

Part II
Cinemas of Ellesmere Port, Heswall, Hoylake, Neston and West Kirby

TABLE OF CINEMAS IN CHRONOLOGICAL ORDER OF OPENING

Date of Opening*	Date of Closing	Map Ref	Cinema	Seating Capacity	Architect
1897(1911)	1932	3	West Kirby Public Hall/ Queens	1500	Keef
1904	1933	6	Hippodrome	—	—
— (1913)	1959	9	Kings (Ellesmere Port)	320	—
1911	present	2	Lighthouse Pavilion/ Winter Gardens/Classic/ Cannon	1000	L.H. Clegg
1912(1916)	1958	4	Kings (Heswall)	1000	A. Shennan
1913	1968	8	Queens (Ellesmere Port)	650	—
1915	1960	1	Kingsway	900	—
1921	1962	5	Neston New Cinema	600	Berry & Co.
1933	1965	3	Tudor	1100	—
1933	1959	7	New Hippodrome	1200	—
1983	present	10	Charles Haywood (EPIC)	174	J.A. Williams

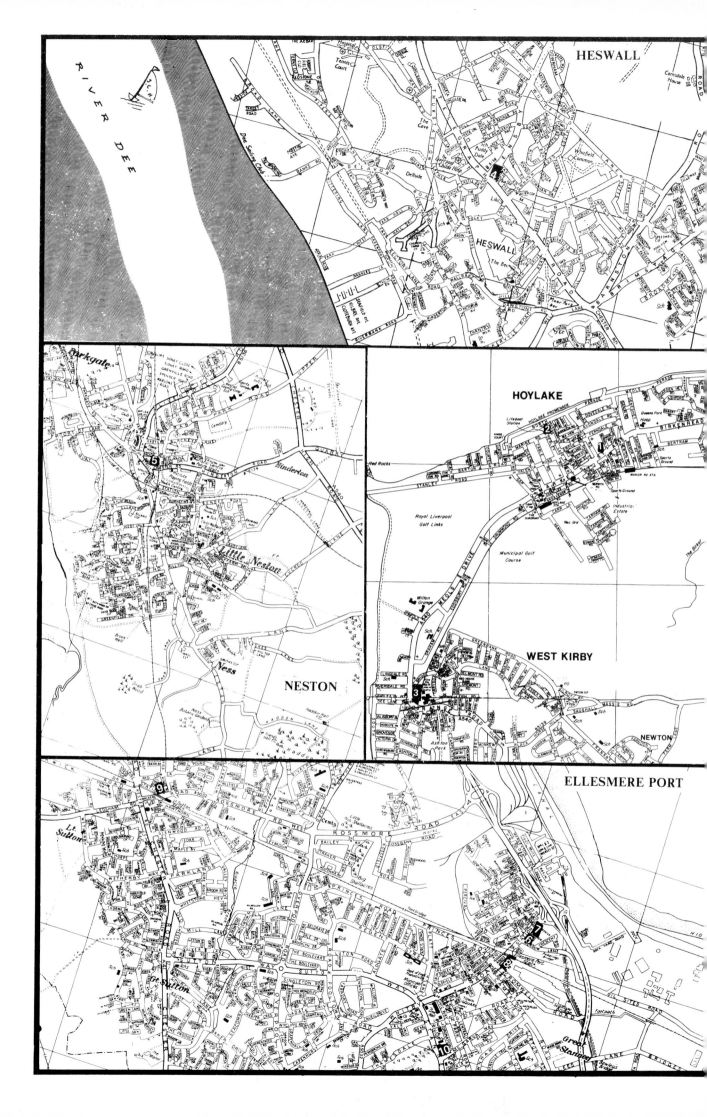

HESWALL

RIVER DEE

HOYLAKE

BIRKENHEAD

Royal Liverpool
Golf Links

Municipal Golf
Course

WEST KIRBY

NEWTON

Parkgate

Little Neston

NESTON

Ness

ELLESMERE PORT

Lt.
Sutton

Gt. Sutton

Charles Haywood Cinema
(EPIC)

Following the closure of the Queens in the late 1960's, Ellesmere Port was left without a cinema. As a result films were shown periodically in the Civic Hall which had been built in the early 1950's. The room used to supervise the lighting in the hall was employed as the projection box. The arrangement was rather haphazard and the programmes were geared mainly to cater for the children of the town. The scheme was well-meaning but the shortcomings of the premises for this purpose were recognised early on. The main use of this superb building was (and remains) for dances, drama production, public and private functions etc., However, as a cinema, the acoustics left much to be desired. The wooden floor was rather noisy and being level did not aid viewing of the screen from the rear of the hall. The seats themselves were of the plastic bucket variety and as such not ideally suited to providing comfortable accommodation for several hours viewing. The large, wide screen was also inadequate and tended to warp in its frame with consequent distortion of the picture. In short, the general atmosphere was clearly not that associated with the more traditional picture-houses. Nevertheless, the Civic Hall did offer an interim cinematographic facility for the town until more appropriate arrangements could be provided.

In 1983 the Ellesmere Port Indoor Centre (EPIC) in McGarva Way, was opened at a cost of around £1,500,000. This complex comprises a swimming pool (which had opened in 1969), sauna, solarium, squash courts, main sports hall (measuring 32m x 26m), a cafeteria, bar, small function rooms and a cinema. The original hope was to include an ice-skating rink and a 0.22 rifle range also but the costs were prohibitive. The centre opened to the public for free viewing on the 30th April 1983, when 5,000 people visited the premises but the cinema had been formally opened a few days earlier on Friday 21st April when the Mayor, Councillor Charles Henning, played host to 300 invited guests, representing industry and voluntary organisations. He congratulated the Borough Architect, Mr. J.A. Williams and his Department for the magnificent job they had done on the project. The cinema was named the Charles Haywood Cinema in tribute to Councillor Haywood, the driving force behind the construction of the complex. Unfortunately, Councillor Haywood was in hospital and, as a result, missed the opening ceremony.

In keeping with the trend for compact cinemas, the 174 seater Epic film theatre, measuring approximately 17m x 14m, is tiny in comparison with the dream palaces of yesteryear. It is a cosy but plainly decorated cinema, designed to double as a lecture theatre, and, whilst there is no stage, it has potential to function as a theatre workshop with the two store-rooms providing possible changing accommodation.

Epic auditorium 1989

Civic . Hall, Ellesmere Port
(1989)

The cinema is located on the third floor of the complex, which itself posed interesting engineering challenges, for example, to construct the raked floor with a 1.5m drop from front to back, and yet retain the integrity of the sports room below. The ceiling design received much attention and the curtain rail and light fittings were well recessed; the mineral fibre ceiling tiles were specially chosen for their acoustic qualities. The screen is fixed on the front wall. The main entrance to the cinema at the rear of the hall is somewhat unusual in being located at the side of the auditorium rather than in the centre as is traditional. The ventilation system is equipped with a complete air handling plant which, although on the same floor as the cinema, is quite remote from the theatre itself. The seats, one of the biggest capital items, were provided by Rank, whilst the electrical work and lighting was undertaken by the local firm of Foord.

ELLESMERE PORT AND NESTON BOROUGH COUNCIL

EPIC CINEMA

WEEKLY SHOWS WILL BE HELD – COMMENCING THURS., 5th MAY, 1983.

* Thursdays and Fridays, 7.30 pm — Adults and accompanied children (subject to certificate).
* Saturday afternoons, 1.30 pm — children's matinees.
* Admission prices: Adults £1.25.
* Senior citizens, children under 16 years and unemployed 70p.

ADULTS   PROGRAMME FOR MAY/JUNE   **MATINEES**

Date	FILM	DATE	FILM
Thurs 5th Fri 6th May	Sylvester Stallone ROCKY III (A)	Sat 14th May	Mickey Rooney, Kelly Reno in BLACK STALLION Plus Shorts and Serial
Thurs 12th Fri 13th May	Paul Newman in FORT APACHE-THE BRONX (AA)	Sat 21st May	CHARLOTTE'S WEB Plus Shorts and Serial
Thurs 19th Fri 20th May	Jeremy Irons, Meryl Streep FRENCH LIEUTENANTS WOMAN (AA)	Sat 28th May	Lloyd Bridges, Lorne Green MISSION GALACTICA (U) Plus Shorts and Serial
Thurs 26th Fri 27th May	Lee Van Cleef, Donald Pleasence, Kurt Russell ESCAPE FROM NEW YORK (AA)	Sat 4th June	GUARDIAN OF THE WILDERNESS Plus Shorts and Serial
Thurs 2nd Fri 3rd June	Jobeth Williams, Craig Nelson in POLTERGEIST (X)	Sat 11th June	GREAT MUPPET CAPER Plus Shorts and Serial
Thurs 9th Fri 10th June	Donald Sutherland, Mary Tyler Moore ORDINARY PEOPLE (AA)	Sat 18th June	PHANTOM TOLLBOOTH Plus Shorts and Serial
Thurs 16th Fri 17th June	Warren Beatty, Diane Keaton REDS (AA)	Sat 25th June	TOM THUMB Plus Shorts and Serial
Thurs 23rd Fri 24th June	Mark Lee, Mel Gibson in GALLIPOLI (A)		To be announced
Thurs 30th Fri 1st July	Jack Lemmon in MISSING (AA)		To be announced

Come and enjoy an evening at the Cinema with licensed bar and cafe facilities.

The projection room at the rear of the auditorium is of respectable dimensions, measuring approximately 6m x 3.5m. Eventually, it was equipped with two 16mm Fumeo projectors and a 35mm Cinemeccancia machine. Just prior to opening of the building, however, there was fierce debate as to whether the £9,000 could be justified for the purchase and installation of the 35mm projector in addition to the two 16mm projectors which had already been provided. It was alleged that part of this expenditure was associated with the provision of a special shutter needed to seal off the projector because of its high heat output, and thereby satisfy fire regulations. The case was made by emphasising how small these on-costs were in comparison with the total outlay on the centre. In line with all parts of the contract, provision of the projection equipment went out to tender and the most attractive offer accepted. Interestingly, when the apparatus arrived and was assembled in the operating room, it needed to be mounted on a wooden platform so that it could be accurately lined-up with the screen. This platform then had to be fitted with hand-rails for safety reasons — a far cry from the standards of design of projection rooms of bygone days, with their cramped conditions and precarious means of access in loft spaces etc.,

The initial arrangements were for film shows on Thursday and Friday evenings with shows especially for children on Saturday afternoons. Admission to the cinema was £1.25 for adults and 70p for children, pensioners and unemployed. Non-members were charged an additional 70p entrance fee to the centre. Nowadays, feature films are screened with full supporting programmes five evenings each week — Friday to Tuesday inclusive. Shows start at 7.30 p.m. (doors open 7.00 p.m.) and persons under sixteen must be accompanied by an adult regardless of the certificate of the film. Admission fees are £1.70 for adults and £1.00 for senior citizens, students, unwaged and accompanied children. Children's matinees are provided each Saturday afternoon when doors open at 1.30 p.m. and the show runs from 2.00 until 3.45 p.m. Admission is only 70p and attendants are always on duty so that children can be left in safety while parents shop or use the sports facilities, although adults are welcome to stay if they so wish. On Monday afternoons senior citizens, retired and disabled persons can enjoy the friendly atmosphere of the film club. A free cup of tea is provided before the show commences at 2.00 p.m., and the programme is arranged with input by the members. Disabled can take their helpers along, whatever their ages. Admission is only 70p, or 95p inclusive of coach transport. In addition, the cinema facilities are made available to the Ellesmere Port Library Film Society who present their film programmes on Thursday evenings at 7.30 p.m. throughout their season mid-October to March. Membership is open to all and guests are welcome.

Epic complex housing the Charles Haywood cinema (1989)

Hippodrome

At the end of 1908 a splendid new building had been erected by the church people at the end of Grosvenor Street, called the Church Institute. Within its first year a maple floor was laid to cater for the new craze of the era — roller skating. The building was also used for social events, meetings, dramas, magic lantern shows and, eventually, moving pictures. However, the first true theatre in Ellesmere Port was Corelli's Hippodrome, built in Meadow Lane a few years earlier in 1904 from corrugated sheets. Although used primarily as a variety theatre, films arrived a few years later with *The Million Mystery*. The pictures were jerky and blotchy, and the reels were continuously breaking down. Nevertheless, they proved to be extremely popular with the audience who paid 1d entrance fee and on the way out they received an orange.

There were two swing-back doors at the front of the building with a beautifully lit cash box. Either side of the theatre there was a balcony which was reached by a ramp, which also gave access to the rear gallery. These long, sloping gangways also led to the exits. The balconies tended to be used most often by the gaily-clad canal people from the long boats and it is reported that these colourful characters provided as much entertainment as the cast. The fire curtain, which was a mosaic of advertisements for local traders, was lowered at the end of each performance and it frequently became stuck half-way which brought howls of laugher from the audience.

In 1926, Mr. T.H. Bate acquired the premises and was granted the license. He encountered no problems in renewing the license in subsequent years until March 1930, when Superintendent Ennion claimed that the Hippodrome was a death trap. The main cause for concern centered around the means of escape

Old Hippodrome undergoing a facelift.

PROGRESS! 23-JULY-1930

from the projection box in the event of fire. The police also thought that the emergency exits from the theatre were too narrow but Mr. Bate contended that the exits were wider than in many more modern cinemas. Also, as a result of the publicity, Mr. Bates claimed that takings had dropped by 25%. In his defence Mr. Bates pointed to reductions in insurance premiums since he had become owner and which were achieved as a result of continuing improvements; insurance costs were £3 3s in 1926, and these had fallen to £1 1s and then to 12/6. After inspection of the premises the magistrates granted the licence on the understanding that certain modifications were carried out within one month. These included replacing the wooden ladder connecting the rewind room and the operating chamber with an iron version fitted with a bulk head. They also took cognizance of the temporary nature of the premises and understood that Mr. Bates was attempting to secure more permanent arrangements.

In 1930 after the Kings and then the Queens had adopted talkies, the Hippodrome was left showing silent films. Their advertisements claimed 'Our Pictures Are Silent But Sound'. They began supplementing their silent movies programmes with variety acts, and posters announced "Real Talking, Singing, Dancing and Music (On Stage)". They also had Laura, emphasising it was a "Talking Parrot". This old established theatre resisted the change until the 1st of June 1931, when the Hippodrome came into line with its counterparts and screened its first talkie *The Unholy Three*, Lon Chaney's only talking success.

The old Hippodrome closed as a cinema and became the Ex-Servicemen's club when a new Hippodrome opened on the 15th of May 1933 in the centre of Ellesmere Port, situated next to the Majestic Ballroom, (which had been built after the 1914-18 war and at one stage showed films using projection from behind the screen) with its facade in Carnegie Street adjacent to the main thoroughfare. It was built by the local company of Thomas Warrington and Sons and, unlike its predecessor in Meadow Lane, it was coorugated iron affair. The frontage was of simple design constructed from sand-faced bricks with blue and cream terracotta finish and an illuminated canopy in blue and gold.

The new Hippodrome (1933)

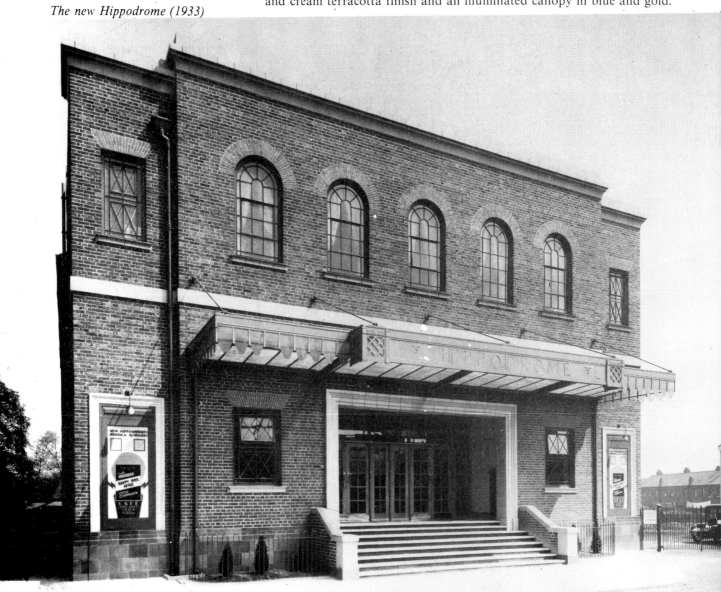

A side entrance with its own pay box provided access to the cheaper front seats but the main entrance was via a broad flight of cream and black terrazzo steps which led from the streets through two pairs of glazed oak doors into a spacious, lofty foyer housing a rather large central cash desk. The foyer floor was covered in black and gold coloured rubber to harmonise with the 'atmospheric' decor. Two wide terrazzo staircases, similar in design to those outside the main entrance, led from the foyer to the balcony and tea room. The latter, tastefully decorated and furnished, was an innovation in Ellesmere Port and use of this amenity was not restricted solely to patrons of the cinema.

The Northern Spray Painting Company Ltd. was employed to treat the internal walls of the Auditorium with gold tints of plastic paint to harmonise with the gold colour acoustic plaster of the curved ceiling. The general colour throughout was greatly enhanced by a system of concealed lighting.

Although the Hippodrome was not equipped with a full theatre stage, a smaller version was provided which, coupled with the very wide illuminated proscenium, afforded facilities for live performances. The 'tabs' were in maroon with stripes and were located behind the flimsy white curtains which were electrically operated with an over-ride facility for manual operation.

The heating and ventilation systems, which proved to be a noticeable feature for visitors from the Queens which was not air conditioned, provided constant movement of fresh air, comfortably warmed in cold weather. The quality and arrangement of the seating added further to the comfort of the audience and provided accommodation for 1,200 people. With the recent advent of talkies the designers were conscious of the need for perfect sound in every part of the cinema and had adopted the latest practice of Honeywill and Stein Ltd., from London, and had installed the latest Western Electric Company talkie equipment. Ample, supervised car-parking facilities were provided for 300 vehicles.

The Hippodrome and the Kings in Little Sutton were under the same management and both began advertising as a B & S Cinema in March 1944. Although the exact date on which the Hippodrome closed is uncertain, the last advertised programme. *Cockleshell Heroes* appeared in June 1959 just at the time that the local newspaper went on strike for a few months. In 1961 the building was converted into a garage.

Mr. G.W. Kirkham, who started as projectionist with the Kings, moved to the Hippodrome in the late 1930's. He recalls that management at the Hippodrome were very keen on timing; programmes started promptly and on one occasion the management installed new seats and carpeting between the end of the matinee and the start of the evening house the same day.

Kings (Little Sutton)

The Kings, formerly the Kings Hall (about which little is known), in Station Road, Little Sutton, Ellesmere Port, opened circa 1913 as a small cinema. The Kings received little attention in the local press but it entered a new lease of life in August 1928 when the management changed to Mrs P. Beattie but by 1931 it was again advertising only periodically in the local press. Messrs. Temperley ands Wallen were the licence holders by 1930 and the County magistrates granted their application for permission to hold a cinematographic performance on Christmas day between 6.00 and 10.00 p.m. The Kings, equipped with two synchronised turntables, introduced talkies to Ellesmere Port on the 24th of March 1930 with a showing of *Mothers Boy* starring Morton Downey. In 1934 the Kings cinema was acquired by the management of the new Hippodrome and was closed for some time for redecoration. It re-opened on the 29th September with the Gracie Fields film *Love, Life and Laughter*. In 1944 the Kings was advertised as a B & S Cinema.

Kings, Little Sutton (1933)

Kings (1950's)

In the early morning hours of Friday the 27th of January 1950, a fire broke out in the Kings and it was some time before the alarm was raised. By the time the fire brigade arrived the blaze was well underway. Mr. Foster, one-time projectionist at the Kings, remembers seeing the interior in ruins the morning after the fire and was devastated by the extent of the damage. One of the two small corner balconies, where it was believed the fire broke out, had collapsed. Flames had spread along the roof, part of which had also caved in, towards the proscenium where they quickly enveloped the stage curtains and screen. Most of the 320 seats were destroyed either by falling, burning debris or as a result of water damage. The operating box and its associated equipment and films, one of which was *The Last Alarm* — a fire services film which had been screened only a few hours previous, were salvaged. Damage was estimated at £4,000.

The premises appear to have remained closed until December the 16th of that year, when it re-opened completely modernised. The changes included provision of a central aisle to replace the side aisles and a slightly increased seating capacity. The small balconies were retained but the seating had been increased to sixteen in each. Also after the fire, two sets of electrically-operated curtains had been installed, one set of red velour and the other light coloured 'flimsy' curtains. The original 6B projectors and BA sound Latern Western Electric system had been replaced by Westar projectors and Westrex Sound Equipment. On the occasion of the re-opening the film was *Easter Parade*.

The exact date of when the Kings closed is uncertain, but it ceased to advertise at the same time that the Hippodrome closed, and the last advertised programme was in June 1959. The building was an eyesore for many years and numerous applications were put forward for its use, e.g. as a social club, a place of worship, car component shop, a timber and glass store and a warehouse; all were refused because of the lack of parking space and on amenity grounds. For a short time in the 1970's the building found use as a recreation centre for youngsters, but the venture folded as a result of complaints by residents about the noise and disturbance. In 1978 a purchase notice was served on the Local Authority and confirmed by the Secretary of State. In the mid 1980's a change of use application for light industry was given permission, but it was never taken up. In 1985, the premises were converted into a health and fitness centre.

Mr. G. Houghton, who joined the cinema as a rewind lad in 1938 before ending up as chief projectionist in the 1950's, remembers visiting the Kings in the silent era and was struck by the red plush bench cheap seats at the front of the cinema.

(before the fire)

(after the fire)

Mr. G.W. Kirkham of Ellesmere Port also remembers working as a projectionist at the Kings in the 1930's for 7/6 per week and later at the Hippodrome where his wages eventually rose to £1 50s for a six day week, working between 10.00 a.m. and 11.00 p.m. In addition to his projection duties, his tasks at the Kings included posting the bills outside the cinema and delivering posters to local public houses. The chief projectionist at the time, Mr. Jack Coats, was simultaneously in charge of the operating room at the Hippodrome. Mr. Kirkham's memories of his early days at the Kings were that it was a particularly small cinema with the screen painted on the back wall, limited stage facilities and manually operated curtains. About four steps led from the street into the foyer which housed a central pay box and stairs to the right and to the left provided access to the small balconies from where one could see directly into the projection room. The latter was a very hot environment, with no windows or ventilation. Next to the projection box was an office containing a telephone and a cool box in which the ice-cream was stored. The maroon velvet seats in the auditorium were arranged on a slightly-raked wooden floor and two emergency exits were provided either side of the hall. The general level of lighting in the auditorium was poor and the exit signs were gas lit. A coke-fired boiler underneath the building was kept lit continuously throughout the winter months. The two usherettes wore maroon uniforms which matched those of their counterparts at the Hippodrome. The rest of the staff comprised Mrs. Harner the cleaner, Mr. Coats, Mr. Kirkham himself as projectionist together with a colleague plus a probationary operator, and the manager Mr. H.N. K. Hudson who also managed the Hippodrome. There was no safe at the Kings and the daily takings were transferred each evening to the Hippodrome. Performances ran continuously each evening, although on Saturdays there were two separate houses at 6.30 and 8.45 p.m. There were matinees on Mondays and Wednesdays with special programmes for children on Saturday afternoons, although Mr. Bobby Foster of Little Sutton recalls that by the time he had started in the projection room at the Kings around 1943 matinees were rarely featured. He also recalls that because of an inadequate means of escape from the projection room, in the event of a fire a hemp rope was provided which, in an emergency, was to be hung through the projection room window to allow staff to escape via the street below. Programmes were changed on Mondays and Thursdays each week. Films were exchanged between the Hippodrome and the Kings and were rushed by van from one cinema to the other while cartoons were screened.

Kings as a gym (1989)

Kings (Heswall)

The Kings Hall in Telegraph Road, Heswall, was built in 1912. In 1914 Sunday Mass was said in Lower Heswall in the ballroom annex of the Victoria Hotel and in the tea room in the gardens of 'Tithebarn', a small-holding owned by Mr. and Mrs. Newsome. By 1916 however, the Kings Hall was considered more suitable and was used by the church for several years. Around this period a Mr. John Pye, who ran the local bus service between Heswall and the top of Singleton Avenue in Prenton, began providing limited cinema entertainments on the premises during certain evenings of the week. Expenditure on programmes however, was governed by the restricted seating capacity and the value of the 'houses'. After some sixteen years with this venture, Mr. Pye realised that more spacious and luxurious facilities could be justified by the rapidly growing population in Heswall and the adjoining districts of Pensby, Barnston, Thurstaston, etc. As a result he embarked on a programme of upgrading the old Kings Hall and to redesign the premises he commissioned the architectural services of Mr. Alfred Shennan of Liverpool (who became one of the foremost designers of cinemas in the region being responsible for, amongst others, the Palladium and Empire in Birkenhead, the Lyceum in New Ferry, The Moreton Picture House, and The Abbey, the Capitol, Carlton, Coliseum, Curzon, Forum, Granada, Mayfair Super, Palladium, Plaza and Regent all in the Liverpool area). Mr. Pye took personal supervision of the transformation which culminated with the opening of the modernised cinema on Christmas Eve, 1928.

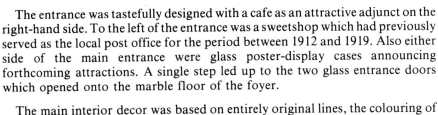

Kings in Telegraph Road

The entrance was tastefully designed with a cafe as an attractive adjunct on the right-hand side. To the left of the entrance was a sweetshop which had previously served as the local post office for the period between 1912 and 1919. Also either side of the main entrance were glass poster-display cases announcing forthcoming attractions. A single step led up to the two glass entrance doors which opened onto the marble floor of the foyer.

The main interior decor was based on entirely original lines, the colouring of the walls and ceilings being a work of art in itself and producing a particularly alluring effect. The painting and decorative work was undertaken by Messrs. Jones and Hough Ltd., of Heswall.

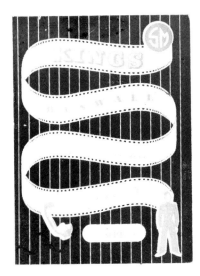

The 900 or so seats in the single storey auditorium were upholstered in orange and red plush and arranged so as to provide maximum comfort. The two side aisles separated the seats into three main blocks. The main central lights were supplemented by a system of wall lights. The stage was spacious and so designed to accommodate an expansive screen which, together with the raked nature of the auditorium floor, ensured that all seats provided an unimpeded view of the pictures. Special attention was devoted to the provision of ample emergency exits both at the rear and at the front of the house.

Kings (circa 1930)

The latest Gaumont type operating plant was installed to provide pictures of acute sharpness and telling effects and Mr. Pye had engaged the services of a select orchestra with a repertoire worthy of the excellent appointments of the new cinema.

The constructional steelwork was undertaken by the Liverpool company of Messrs. Thomas Jones, while the electrical contract was awarded to Messrs. W.M.H. Atherton and Co., of Heswall. Messrs. Lee and Sons of Liverpool, installed the heating and ventilation system, "upon which the reputation of any building of this character must necessarily depend". However, this equipment seems not to have lived up to expectations and Mr. Bryant of Eastham, a regular patron of the Kings in the 1930's and 40's, recalls how inefficient the heating was in winter and remembers with 'bitter' experience that "if you went in cold you came out freezing." A separate ballroom existed upstairs.

Mr. Pye adopted a catholic policy aimed at providing a wide choice of entertainment so as to attract the largest possible audience. Ample car parking facilities were provided for those patrons wishing to motor to the cinema, whilst for others, buses ran from the outlying district to suit the various times of the performances which originally were at 7.45 p.m. on Mondays, Tuesdays, Thursdays and Fridays, and at 2.45 p.m., 6.30 p.m. and 8.30 p.m. on Wednesdays and Saturdays. Admission charges, including tax, were 4d, 6d, 1/3, 1/6 and 2/4 and seats could be booked in advance at no extra charge. The opening performance, which was attended by a large appreciative crowd, included *The Magic Flame*, a film masterpiece starring the two screen lovers Ronald Colman and Vilma Banky, supported by a serial and topical subjects.

Mr. Bryant also remembers queueing in the side road for entrance to the front stalls which had their own access and pay box.

In the mid-thirties the cinema became part of the Liverpool based Stanley Grimshaw Circuit and later Byrom Picture Houses Ltd., but by 1946, it was part of the SM Super Cinemas circuit up to the time when they sold out to Essoldo in 1954. Interestingly, during the war the cinema was used as a centre for issuing ration books.

By 1958, the building was up for sale. An attempt to auction the premises with vacant possession of the cinema and ballroom but with the two adjoining shops let, failed to realise the reserve price of more than £7,500 and the offer was withdrawn. Later in the year plans for alterations and improvements to the Kings had been submitted to Wirral Councils Town Planning Committee who recommended approval subject to certain conditions. It was understood that the proposals were to level the floor and change its use from cinema to that of a multiple store but to retain the ballroom. Eventually the building was indeed converted into a Tesco store and more recently this has changed hands.

An Essoldo

KINGS
HESWALL
Telephone: Heswall 81

MARCH 1955
Evenings continuous from 5.45 p.m.
Children's Matinee (Saturday)

93

Kingsway

Prior to the opening of the Kingsway cinema in Market Street, Hoylake on Saturday, 10th July 1915, local people had to be content with watching irregular film shows at the Hoylake Institute (later the YMCA) or the Central Hall. With an elaborate decor and seating capacity for 900, the Kingsway soon became one of the popular picture houses on Wirral. The opening performance was a showing of *Jane Shore* with admission charges ranging from 3d to 1/- or 7/6 for a box.

Sound pictures arrived in April 1930 and in 1934 the cinema underwent a complete modernisation programme to improve heating, revamp the offices and lounge and to increase the seating capacity by another 200.

A particularly striking feature of the 1934 modernisation scheme was the two large rectangular metal-framed light fittings with frosted glass that were fitted flush to the ceiling and smaller fittings of similar design on the side walls. These contained both white and red lamps and were wired on two circuits in order that the white bulbs could be dimmed prior to commencement of the show, yet allow the red lamps to remain on until the titles of the first film had faded from the screen.

The stage was illuminated by footlights and an overhead batten, each wired on three circuits, though normally a combination of orange and red was used with the orange circuit being dimmed at the same time as the white house-lights. The main stage curtain was of cream-coloured satin, surmounted by a shaped pelmet in green with red trim. This curtain was electrically operated, but a second set of hand-operated festooned curtains could be drawn across the screen when the stage was used.

Kingsway (1935)

Kingsway foyer (1935)

Kingsway auditorium and balcony (1935)

Kingsway (1935)

The general tone of the colour scheme was one of cream and yellow outside, with cream, green and red internal decor. The balcony was noticeably shallow and both the ceiling and proscenium were stepped. Outside the main entrance, glass showcases advertised forthcoming attractions. On entering the Kingsway in the early 1940's one could hardly fail to notice the strong, sweet odour of disinfectant that pervaded the air from the moment you set foot in the cinema. Also, very noticeable were the non-stop renditions of popular 'hit' records that preceded the show, contrasting rather unfavourably with the tuneful light orchestral records to be heard at most other 'better class' cinemas in those days. Saturday matinees were especially popular and despite the increased capacity the HOUSE FULL sign was often used. Interestingly, the Kingsway was one of the few cinemas that did not hold childrens' matinees, but apparently the management were relaxed at admitting children unaccompanied by adults. In an attempt to compete with the modern cinemas on the Wirral, such as the Ritz, an ambitious investment programme to upgrade the Kingsway was planned, including provision for Cinemascope. Ironically, it was this £15,000 alteration programme that cost the picture-house its life when the bank foreclosed the loan and the building had to be sold to pay off the debt.

On March 12th 1960, the Kingsway closed to a performance of 'Blue Jeans' starring Carol Lynley and Brandon de Wilde and soon after the building was demolished to make way for a supermarket and shops.

Lighthouse Pavilion

(Winter Gardens/Classic/Canon)

Hoylake in the late 1800's boasted two lighthouses, a Lower Lighthouse and an almost identical, but taller, Upper Lighthouse in Valentia Road.

In 1908 the Lower Lighthouse extinguished its light for ever and the following year it, together with the ajoining coast-guard house and grounds, was acquired by Mr. Frank Wolsey and converted into a somewhat temporary pavilion for summer concert parties, reviews and pierrot shows. In 1910 more permanent premises were designed by L.H. Clegg. The new, rather irregular trapezium-shaped building, tapered in towards the stage. The latter was 19 ft. 6 in. deep and 35 ft. to the top of the flies finished with a 30 ft x 17 ft 6 in. proscenium arch which closely resembled that of the Central Hall built the previous year. The coast-guard house (built in 1866 and the profile of which can still be seen to this day) formed the basis for the new foyer and office. The most distinguishing feature, however, was the entrance through the ground floor of the lighthouse itself. Interestingly, pay boxes were also provided in the front exit passages for use by patrons using the pit. The 1,000 seats were located on a single raked floor; only the first two rows had tip-up seats.

After some delay, the Lighthouse Pavilion eventually opened on 31st August, 1911. Throughout its long history the Lighthouse experienced many changes in ownership and management and periods of closure. The first change came in 1917 when Frank Wolsey "joined the colours". It re-opened for brief periods the following year, still as a variety theatre under the management of H. Bishop, and closed again in May 1919. Although the bioscope had featured in the programmes dating back to November 1911, the building only became a cinema proper on the 14th June 1920, when it re-opened as the Pavilion Super Cinema with Tom Moore starring in *Go West Young Man*. The supporting film was the

The Lighthouse Pavilion (circa 1918)

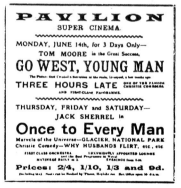

Christie comedy 'Three Hours Late' with musical accompaniment provided by a 'first-class orchestra'. Admission at 9d, 1/3, 1/10 and 2/4 was rather expensive for the day. The local press at the time reported, somewhat theatrically, that "The old 'Lighthouse' has passed away; at last the caterpillar has blossomed forth into a radiant butterfly" and the papers made great play of the new white roof of elaborate design, the artistically-panelled walls and the high quality of the seats. The new roof, however, was nothing more than another ceiling with imitation beams hiding the flimsy horizontal struts, but whilst probably improving the acoustics and heating when compared with the original pitched roof, it obscured the top of the proscenium arch for all but those in the front rows.

In 1921, the licence changed hands on several occasions, first in March to Harry Humphries, then in May to Gordon Dudley West and again in October to Alfred Rowland. Initially during this period, cine-variety was the attraction, but when the theatre closed in November 1922, live entertainment ceased.

Unfortunately, in 1932 the old lighthouse part of the building was demolished as part of a plan to erect the "Empress Ballroom" (a building in fact which never materialised). The present entrance in Alderley Road was then added and on the 22nd January 1923, the establishment re-opened as the Winter Gardens variety theatre under the management of L.C. King and direction of F.V. Ross (previously with the Tivoli, New Brighton). The Winter Gardens closed in April for the proposed construction of the ballroom on the car park at the rear of the building, but when it was realised that this project was to be shelved the theatre re-opened on the 9th June 1923. During the next couple of years, the lease again changed hands and while it was with the owners of the Kingsway and Queens cinemas, the premises remained closed for most of the time. The licence transferred again in 1927 and the theatre was used for both pictures and variety, with innovations such as matinees for ladies only. Films continued to be included in programmes until 1928 when live shows became the main feature under the management of Mr. Alfred Rutherford. When the licence was due for renewal in 1930 he was under close scrutiny regarding the distribution of leaflets publicising the play *One Man's Woman*. The Police had considered the literature offensive and had ordered that no further copies be circulated.

By April 1930, F.V. Ross again took a controlling interest with Mr. Joe Vernmon as manager. Until January 1931 when Messrs. Walmesley, Heap and Parkinson became the proprietors, films were dropped from the programme as a deliberate and well-advertised policy. After a further short period of closure, the Winter Gardens re-opened on the 9th February 1931, with cine-variety shows. With talkies well established at the neighbouring cinemas it was surprising that the Winter Gardens chose to continue only with silent films. This judgement proved to be suspect and the last silent movie *Master and Man* starring Henry de Vrus was shown just two months later on Saturday the 18th of April. The cinema re-opened on the 11th of May 1931 with "the latest talkie installation" and the first film was *Women Everywhere* featuring Fifi Dorsay and J. Harold Murray.

Competition between the local picture houses during the next few years became fierce, with further changes in administration at the Winter Gardens. The burning down of Queens cinema in West Kirby in 1932 provided the chance for the Winter Gardens to attract extra custom, an opportunity not missed by the management who provided buses to take last-house patrons back to West Kirby. When the Queens was replaced by the Tudor the following year, advertisements for the Winter Gardens emphasized their superior ventilation system, luxury seats and new stage curtains. Other attractions included provision of free hot water in the car park for patron's cars and a new decorative scheme which was being undertaken "slowly, in order to obviate offensive paint odours". It is also of interest to note that the admission charges of 6d, 9d, 1/- and 1/3 in 1934 were considerably less than in 1920.

The SM Super Cinema circuit, which owned many picture houses throughout the country including the Ritz in Birkenhead, in 1940 took over the Winter Gardens' lease and later the freehold. Mr. Shalless became manager and he soon replaced the poor projection and sound equipment. Extensive publicity resulted in excellent attendances. Throughout the war years, the theatre was used primarily as a cinema in the evenings and as a venue for training troops during the day. Live shows were introduced on Sundays.

At the direction of the local council, the old coastguard projection room, which was a cramped wooden-floored enclosure above the foyer with inadequate emergency escape facilities, was extended in 1951 and modernised.

Reconstruction after the fire (1976)

Cannon exterior (1980's)

The room was re-roofed and the projectors, previously sited at the Alderley Road side of the building, were relocated centrally in the more-spacious new projection suite. With the decline in the cinema business, the SM Company sold their 'houses' to the Essoldo group in 1954. Despite various attempts to attract audiences the capacity of the three picture houses in the West Kirby and Hoylake area was far in excess of the demand and, being on the sea front and some distance from the centre of activity the Hoylake Winter Gardens (along with the Winter Gardens in New Brighton) was the first of three to close on the 3rd of January 1959, with a showing of *No Time for Sergeants* starring Myron McCormick. Mr. Arthur Shalless retired.

For most cinemas this would have represented the final chapter in their history but not so for the Winter Gardens. Thus, when the nearby Kingsway closed in 1960, Essoldo repainted the Winter Gardens and in May of that year re-opened it on a trial basis with a showing of Mario Lanza's *For The First Time*. Business was disappointing and closure was again imminent but for a petition by

The interior 1980's

staff which gained the cinema a reprieve. Arthur Shalless was tempted out of retirement, an action which resulted in improved box-office takings and the Winter Gardens went on to out-survive the Tudor, which closed in 1965. A couple of years later, the unreliable old coke boiler was replaced by an oil-fired version and the auditorium was re-seated, but with a reduced capacity of just 380. Arthur Shalless continued in control prior to retiring for the last time in 1971, when he was replaced by William Goodwin, formerly with the Essoldo (Queens) in Ellesmere Port. Essoldo then sold out to Classic Cinemas in March 1972, and a programme of renovation commenced which included installation of new toilets and carpets, the removal of the old gas secondary lighting system, combining the pay box and kiosk into a single unit, remodelling of the entrance foyer and tiling of the front steps, plus a redecoration throughout. In 1973 the cinema was renamed the Classic.

Trouble struck on the 11th of January, when fire broke out in the early hours, probably as a result of a smouldering cigarette. Damage originally estimated at £2,000 was thought to be superficial, but on more careful inspection it resulted in the closure of the cinema for some time whilst the ceiling was replaced and considerable redecoration and electrical rewiring work was undertaken. New seats, carpeting and flooring were needed, along with screen and stage curtains. Costs eventually exceeded £11,000. Ironically the first casualty in the programme was 'Towering Inferno' with Steve McQueen. The cinema re-opened on Sunday the 14th of March, with the film 'Great Expectations'.

The last decade or so has been relatively uneventful and, despite proposals for the conversion of the building into a full-time bingo hall, the Classic has outlived many of its more distinguished rivals and to this day continues to provide film entertainment as the Cannon.

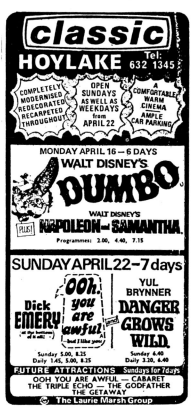
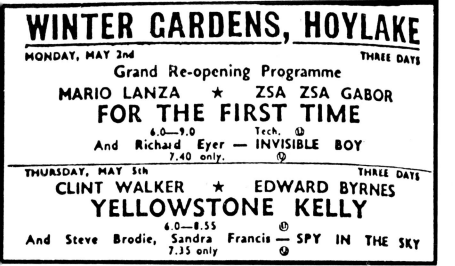

Neston New Cinema
(Royal Cinema)

Films were first shown in Neston circa 1912 by the Neston Electric Picturedrome Company at the Institute, Hinderton Road, which became known as Maxwell's Picturedrome. The shows were on Mondays, Wednesdays and Saturdays 'prompt' at 7.45 p.m., and the films were rarely advertised as a result of which patrons usually did not know in advance which films were to be screened; the only certainty was the serial. The films were supported by live acts and prices at this time were 3d and 6d. During the first World War the Institute was converted into a military hospital and in 1915 the cinema was transferred to the Town Hall. Again the programmes received no advanced publicity and the wooden seats were rather uncomfortable. Pictures continued to be shown there for almost a decade until more permanent facilities were provided.

The first proposal for a purpose-built cinema in Neston was to construct one in Parkgate Road. However, it was the planning application, submitted by Captain George Alan and Mr. Norman Glegg, for a picture house in Chester Road that was eventually passed by Neston Council on the 19th April 1920. Edward Berry and Co., of Liverpool produced plans in May to obtain a licence from the Neston magistrates. The plans were for seating for 508 persons, with 88 in the gallery. A row of cottages and a woodyard were demolished and the building by a Heswall concern commenced in June of that year. The opening of the Neston New Cinema took place on the 18th of April 1921, with a showing of *The Temporary Gentleman* starring Owen Nares and Madge Titheradge, when the management invited local residents to two performances. On both occasions, packed houses resulted. The manager at the time was J.F. Tillston. By the end of

Royal standing derelict (1960's)

the week, the main attraction was *Night Riders* with Albert Ray. During the week performances were continuous between 6.30 p.m. and 10.20 p.m., with houses on a Saturday at 6.15 and 8.30 p.m. and a children's matinee starting at 2.30 p.m. Prices in the early days were somewhat high at 2/6 in the balcony and between 5d and 1/6 in the stalls with half price fees for the children's matinee.

No expense had been spared in the design of the picture house and it was claimed to be one of the most up-to-date de-luxe establishments in the area. Two sets of steps, separated by a small garden, led up to a central entrance outside of which posters advertised the programme, itself somewhat of an innovation in Neston. The entrance led into a spacious and well proportioned hall of pleasing design from which two sets of stairs gave access to the small balcony. The auditorium had a seating capacity of around 400, with seats so arranged on a raked floor, that even the largest of hats would pose no problems in viewing the screen. Seats from the cheapest to the most expensive were of upholstered tip-up style and they were laid out in three rows, with two aisles separating the side rows from the main central block. The proscenium was of novel lines with pictures being projected from a box at the back of the balcony on to the screen on the back wall. There was a very small stage which was used occasionally for amateur dramatics. there were no curtains of any significance.

Special attention was paid to the ventilation of the building and the main auditorium lighting was provided by large ceiling electroliers supplemented by a number of side lamps. The decor of the passages was in harmony with that of the interior as a whole.

Mr. J.F. Tillston had previous experience in picture houses in Liverpool and the Lake District and records indicate his involvement up until 1928. By February 1929, a Mr. Robert F. Dansie had become manager. However, his reign was short lived. When he applied for an extension to his temporary music, singing and dancing licence the police objected because of certain irregularities at the cinema. Unbeknown to Mr. Dansie, the police had called in on The New Cinema on several occasions between 9.00 and 10.00 p.m. when they found no one in attendance other than the projectionist. Despite claims by the manager that he had only been absent for five to ten minutes, the magistrates were concerned that no one would have been in charge in the event of a fire at the premises. They dismissed as unacceptable, Mr. Dansie's argument that the projectionist would have taken charge of the situation. As a result, the extension was refused and the cinema was without music for a while until the situation was resolved when, before the month was out, the proprietors appointed Mr. James Frazier Daniel of Neston as manager.

The Cheshire Directories for 1934 and 1939 fail to name a manager, but the proprietors were given as Major J.F. Burns and Mrs. Marie Clegg. Around 1940 the managing director was Mr. H.S. Baylis and the cinema was advertised as under the same management as The Pola (Welshpool), The Plaza (Dolgelly), Pavillion (Llandrindod Wells), The Regent ((Newtown), The Crescent (Penmaenmawr), The Regal (Beaumaris) and The Prince of Wales (Holywell). One of the last managers was Mr. Doran.

Mr. Charlie Bell, now living in Chirk, recalls as a young projectionist at the New Cinema, charging up batteries for patrons, including the local registrar and the bank manager.

Mr. Tom Johnson of Raby Cottage, Neston, remembers the musical arrangements in the early days. Initially, a pianist played alone in a curtained-off area to the side of the stage; Mr. Maine Edwards was followed as pianist by Mr. Boustead. Then in 1923 at the age of fifteen, Tom Johnson earned 7s 6d for playing for the Friday night and Saturday matinee performances. By 1924 he was earning £2 10s for playing six nights and Saturday afternoon. His wages were later reduced to £2 because the cinema was not paying and at the same time, admission charges were reduced to 1/3 in the balcony and 6d, 9d and 1/- in the stalls. Between about 1925 and 1928 the cinema had a small orchestra comprising Bob Hughes (a grocer) on drums, Neville Scott (clerk), Vince Prosser (plasterer or bricklayer) and Billy Baker of the Chester Arms all on violin. Marjory Scott on cello occasionally accompanied the quartette. By this time, Tom Johnson had left to study at Manchester, but together with his sister, they provided some temporary cover on Friday nights. When the manager was absent, as was often the case, a violinist stood in for him.

Although the cinema had indoor toilets, this did not inhibit the children; during the matinee an added hazard to the musicians was the stream of urine that

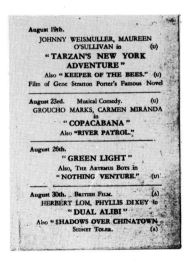

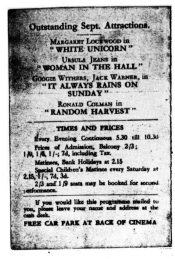

103

flowed down the sloping floor. The children squatted where they would and then changed places so as not to be found out by the management.

Clearly, with the arrival of the talkies in 1930, the musical accompaniments gradually became redundant; a Panatrope was installed and for a while a pianist and a violinist were retained to provide musical interludes between films. One local resident complained to the council about the noise nuisance resulting from the installation of the sound apparatus, but this was ruled not to be council business and no more was heard of the complaint.

The New Cinema had an uneventful history. It closed on the 23rd April 1960, with the screening of Peter Sellers' *I'm Alright Jack*. Since its closure plans were prepared to convert the premises into a non-residential club but these were abandoned and the lease was acquired by Mr. G.B. Taylor of Rullerton Road, Wallasey who also ran the Royal Cinema, Wallasey. After some modernisation, the picture house re-opened on the 13th of November 1961, this time as the Royal Cinema. The main feature of the gala re-opening was Walt Disney's *Pollyanna* starring Hayley Mills, actress daughter of star John Mills and his playwright wife, Mary Hayley Bell. Councillor Walter Bruce, Chairman of Neston Council and representatives of several of the major film rental companies were amongst the invited guests. The seating capacity had been increased slightly to accommodate 450 people. Following a poll in favour of the opening of the cinema on Sundays, in June 1962 Parliament approved an order extending the Sunday Cinema Act to Neston and urban district but this failed to keep the Royal in existence and it closed for good soon after, falling victim to vandals and fire. It was then used as a bingo hall for a while, and after refurbishment it opened as a shopping arcade on the 8th of November 1984.

Seen at the re-opening on Monday of the Neston Cinema, now re-named the Royal Cinema, are, left to right: Mr. and Mrs. G. B. Taylor, Councillor Walter Bruce, chairman of Neston Council, and Mrs. Bruce, Mr. H. V. Rowland, who is a partner in the project, with Mr. and Mrs. Taylor, and Mr. Frank Jordan, of G. B.-Kalee, suppliers of the projection equipment.

Photo by Alban Knox.

Queens (Ellesmere Port)

The Ellesmere Port and District Cinema Co. Ltd. was floated in 1913 for the erection of a cinema but nothing appears to have come of this. However, a similar venture by The Ellesmere Port Picture Palace Co. was more successful. This was founded on the basis of a purchase agreement for a small site in Whitby Road, costing £960 and to construct a picture palace for £2,950. The scheme was devised by the 3 corn and flour merchants, Mr. W.W. Scott of Wallasey, Mr. J. Scott of Liscard and Mr. G. Walton of Liverpool, plus Mr. W. Green, a Wallasey draper. In July 1913, Mr. A.M. Dutton, on behalf of the proprietors of the new Queens picture house in Whitby Road, was granted a cinematographic licence and the premises opened next to Baines' pawnshop soon after. The silent pictures were accompanied by a trio of imported musicians. This represented an important improvement in the standards of entertainment in Ellesmere Port. Prior to the Queens, people had to sit on forms and chairs at the Co-op Hall or the Church Institute but at the Queens they could sit in somewhat more comfort in more pleasant surroundings with capacity for around 650 patrons.

The opening date was displayed at the front of the building high above the entrance where it remains prominent to this day. A small flight of steps led from the street into the cinema foyer. Inside, facing the main entrance, was the pay box. Doors either side of the pay booth provided access to the auditorium, the ceiling of which was steeply curved and ornate. Two narrow curved staircases led from the foyer to a small mezzanine lounge from where a short flight of half moon steps led up to the balcony. Plush seats were provided for the "toffs" and hard wooden benches for 2d and 4d customers. It was a neck-breaking task to watch the films from the cheaper seats but still a fascinating experience in the early pioneering days.

Queens (1950's)

Queens as a bingo hall (1989) the balcony and ceiling though redecorated have undergone little change

On the 19th of February 1930, Mr. Wallace, on behalf of Timperley and Wallace, applied for an extension of their licence to enable pictures to be screened from 2.00 to 11.00 p.m. Mr. Wallace explained that they intended to show talking pictures and that the operating costs associated with running a talkie hall were considerably greater than those for showing silent films. Furthermore, the anticipated demand resulting from this new venture would exceed their current capabilities, (at the time Ellesmere Port residents were travelling to Birkenhead, Chester and Liverpool to experience the talkie phenomenon). Indeed, the Queens planned to expand their staff by five to help cope with the expected demand. It was also argued that the extended hours would be more amenable to the growing numbers of shift workers. The last silent film screened at the Queens featured Jean Hersholt and Lina Basquette in *The Younger Generation*, a story of a family united by poverty and divided by wealth. On the 4th of April 1930, the Queen's talkie premiere was the all singing and dancing *The Rainbow Man* with Eddie Dowling and featuring the songs 'Sleepy Valley', 'Little Pal' and 'The Rainbow Man'. When the talkies arrived the prices were 4d in the pit and 1/3 in the balcony. Equipment consisted of Ernemann II projectors and BTH sound apparatus. One set of crimson velour curtains were hand operated from within the projection room. The stage was lit by footlight and batten with automatic colour change on the stage lighting.

In 1933 the Queens underwent some internal improvements. The balcony was re-seated with red plush semi-tub chairs and re-carpeted with red material of sound absorbent pile. The ground floor was similarly treated and new seats were installed at the rear of the auditorium, whilst the forms at the front were replaced by tip-up seats. New decorative lights were fitted and further modifications included the construction of French doors onto the balcony to eliminate draught.

By 1941 St. George Ltd. had become the proprietors and in 1944 the Queens was advertised as an SM Cinema and came under Essoldo control in 1954. Patrons of the early days can remember the projectionist, Mr. Samuel Rowley, regularly bringing a ladder on to the balcony to climb up and wipe mist from the projection room windows. The cinema closed for extensive alteration in November 1968, when Bingo was gaining in popularity. The last advertised film was *The Green Berets,* starring John Wayne, and at the time of its closure the manager was Mr. W. Morgan. This was Ellesmere Port's last cinema for the town's 45,000 population. Since re-opening in the late 1960's, the Queens has been used as a Bingo Hall although the projection room has been retained and the balcony remains virtually unaltered, although the main auditorium has been refitted, and the premises have expanded into what was the pawnshop.

Tudor

After the Queens at West Kirby had been destroyed by fire in 1932, the site, at the corner of Bridge Street and Grange Road, was acquired by Kemp and Wilkinson Cinemas of Nottingham. The Tudor cinema was designed by Mr. A.J. Thraves and built by J.H. Metcalf Bros. The 1,100 seat cinema was officially opened by Mr. J.J. MacLaren, Chairman of the Council, on Monday the 4th of December 1933, and was named the Tudor because of its characteristic Tudor-styled facade: a half-timbered gable surmounted a well-proportioned oriel window with decorative panels underneath. Above the window, the name of the theatre was displayed in Olde English lettering, finished in red and superimposed with Neon tubing. The only other illumination on the frontage was supplied by two antique-type circular lanterns with leaded glass.

The interior, although designed on modern lines, did not clash with the period treatment of the exterior. The decorations were in quiet tones, part of the walls being rough-cast and fading from tangerine at the base to ivory at the ceiling. The main walls carried a touch of ornamentation in the form of large blue and silver frames, inside which the colours of the plastic paint, mainly tangerine and green, had been rubbed to enhance the shading.

The seating was upholstered in moquetté of futuristic design, whilst floor coverings were in plain grey carpeting edged with red. Heavy Wilton carpet runners in bright design, covered the stairs to the balcony. Three octagonal fibrous plaster features adorned the ceiling and concealed the lamps for the main auditorium lighting and ventilation extract grilles.

Tudor (1933)

Unlike the Kingsway, which was owned by the same company, the Tudor had a large circle but no fly tower and the stage was the original stage from the Queens. Two Kalee No.8 Projectors were used in the operating booth, with Western Electric 3A sound equipment with a Hewittic rectifier. The manager at the time was Mr. A.H. Charot and the opening film was *Night of the Garter* starring Sydney Howard (who sent a telegram of good wishes for the opening) with *So This is Harris's* as the support film. Seat prices ranged from 6d for the front stalls to 2s 4d in the front circle.

A well-remembered feature of this cinema were the heavy gold coloured satin stage curtains with their attractive appliquéd design which, unfortunately, were destroyed after a fire that damaged the stage towards the end of 1949. But for the keen sense of smell and prompt action of a young policeman the fire may have been allowed to develop further and the Tudor may have suffered the same fate as the Queens on the same site sixteen years earlier. So popular was this cinema that several patrons offered contributions towards the cost of replacing the drapes.

Following the well-respected Queens was a difficult task, but the Tudor soon became popular and the 'House Full' sign was often used — audience numbers being boosted during the early 1940's by evacuees in the area. It became necessary to arrive at the Tudor at least 30 minutes early in order to get a seat! Immediately after the war the Tudor was used for more varied forms of entertainment including performances by visiting orchestras (such as the Liverpool Philharmonic Orchestra (1948) and the BBC Northern Orchestra) and pantomimes which were renowned throughout the peninsula.

In 1951 ownership of the Tudor passed from K & W Cinemas to the Southport based Spring Theatres (Cheshire) Ltd., Following the pattern of declining box offices in the rest of Wirral, the Tudor cinema closed on the 30th of January 1965 with *Seance On A Wet Afternoon* featuring Kim Stanley and Richard Attenborough.

After a few years usage as a Bingo Hall, Kent and Thanet Casinos Ltd., took over the property, re-naming it the Legalite Casino Club. The Tudor was sold again in 1974 and it is currently run as Bridge Walk Business Centre.

Tudor foyer (1933)

Tudor – view from balcony (1933)

Tudor – auditorium and balcony (1933)

West Kirby Public Hall

(Queens)

This Public Hall was built by the West Kirby Public Hall and Estate Co. Ltd., (with Mr. William Alfred Jones as Chairman and managing director) in 1897 in Grange Road on the site previously occupied by railwaymen's cottages. It was designed in the free Renaissance style by Mr. Keef. The foyer entrance in the 140 ft long frontage, was flanked either side by a tower 75 ft high. The luxuriously carpeted 80 ft x 50 ft auditorium had a seating capacity of 1,500. It was surrounded by wide corridors, above which were gold ornamented side balconies. It sported a large orchestra pit and a stage measuring 50 ft in width and 21 ft in depth, which was used by many famous variety artistes. A marble floor was added in 1908 so that the building could be used for roller skating, a popular craze at the time.

Three years later on the 17th of July, 'Living Pictures' were shown by the London Bioscope Company at prices ranging from 3d to 1/-. From the 26th of December 1911, Messrs. George Fenton and Victor Branford presented a week of films in the Hall, making the premises the first permanent cinema in the region when they secured the lease for the Hall the following year. It opened on the 4th of March 1912, with Mr. Ernest Price as manager. The lease transferred to Mr. Leonard Clegg in 1917, possibly while Messrs. Fenton and Branford were on active service but, during this time, problems were encountered with the projectors and on several occasions the local papers carried apologies and "hoped that the trouble is now at an end". George Fenton resumed control with Stanley Rogers in May 1918 and continued to present pictures until the lease expired in November 1921 when the Public Hall was sold to the Kingsway Picture House (Hoylake) Ltd.,

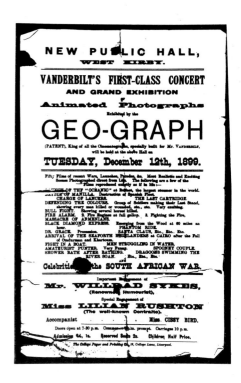

A handbill dated Tuesday, 12th December 1899, for a show at the New Public Hall, West Kirby. Films shown included products by Edison, Lumiere and Warwick Trading Company.

The foyer of West Kirby's public hall, built in 1899 and considered, at the time, to be one of the finest halls in Wirral. In later years it became the Queens Picture House.

Fire gutted the Queens Picture House in 1932. From its ashes rose the Tudor Cinema which, when it opened on 4th December 1933, provided seated accommodation for 1,100 patrons.

The Hall closed on the 3rd of December and the premises were extensively refurbished by the new management. The cinema, however, re-opened as the Queens at 7.30 p.m. on Christmas Eve 1921, just three weeks after closing! During this time the building had been re-seated, re-heated, re-decorated and thoroughly modernised. Gershom Stewart Esq., MP for Wirral, was in attendance for the occasion and he recalled how unlucky the year had proved to be, noting that the sum of 1921 was 13! He went on to wish everyone a Merry Christmas before the film of Mrs. Humphrey Ward's *Lady Rose's Daughter* was shown. All the proceeds were donated to local charities, such as the Distress Committee's fund and the War Memorial fund for soldiers' dependents. Throughout the following week, the programme consisted of live entertainment which included a delightful musical stage play entitled *The Magic Melody* specially composed by the Musical Director, Mr. F.J. Wilson. In the afternoon and evening film shows were screened starting with Douglas Fairbanks in *The Mark of Zorro* and Harold Lloyd in *His Royal Slyness*. Musical accompaniment was provided by a 'grand orchestra' and admission was at 7d in the pit stalls and 1s 6d in the circle. *The Love Trap* was the last silent picture to be shown on Saturday the 26th of April 1930 and the first talking picture was *Broadway Melody* which was presented on the 28th of April 1930, using the "all British, world's best, BTH sound producer".

The story of the Queen's was brought to an abrupt end in the early hours of Sunday the 28th of February 1932, when a spectacular fire destroyed the building. The ruins presented a sad sight as gaunt, blackend walls looked down on an interior of twisted metal and piled-up refuse. When the Fire Brigade arrived at 5.00 a.m., the interior of the building was already a raging inferno and clearly beyond salvage. The fire-fighters' main aim became prevention of fire spreading to adjoining property including the Legion Hall and St. Andrew's Institute. Despite their endeavours and use of 60,000 — 70,000 gallons of water per hour, smoke soon billowed from the windows and under the eaves of the Institute. The final programme the evening before the disaster was *The Hound of the Baskervilles*.

OTHER TITLES FROM COUNTYVISE

Local History

Birkenhead Priory..Jean McInniss
Birkenhead Park...Jean McInniss
The Spire is Rising..Dorothy Harden
The Search for Old Wirral..David Randall
Neston and Parkgate..Jeffrey Pearson
Scotland Road ....Terry Cooke
Helen Forrester Walk ....K. Rickard
Women at War ....Pat Ayres
Merseyside Moggies..R.M. Lewis
Dream Palaces...Harold Ackroyd
Forgotten Shores ....Maurice Hope
Cheshire Churches ....Roland W. Morant
Storm over the Mersey ....Beryl Wade
Memories of Heswall 1935 — 1985 ....Heswall W.E.A.

Local Railway Titles

Seventeen Stations to Dingle..John W. Gahan
The Line Beneath the Liners...John W. Gahan
Steel Wheels to Deeside...John W. Gahan
Seaport to Seaside..John W. Gahan
Northern Rail Heritage..K. Powell and G. Body
A Portrait of Wirral's Railways ....Roger Jermy

Local Shipping Titles

Sail on the Mersey ....Michael Stammers
Ghost Ships on the Mersey..K.J. Williams
The Liners of Liverpool – *Part I*...Derek Whale
The Liners of Liverpool – *Part II*..Derek Whale
The Liners of Liverpool – *Part III*...Derek Whale
Hands off the Titanic ....Monica O'Hara
Mr. Merch and other stories..Ken Smith

Local Sport

The Liverpool Competition (Local Cricket)..................................P.N. Walker
Lottie Dcd..Jeffrey Pearson

History with Humour

The One-Eyed City...Rod Mackay
Hard Knocks...Rod Mackay
The Binmen are coming ....Louis Graham

Natural History

Birdwatching in Cheshire ....Eric Hardy

Other Titles

Speak through the Earthquake, Wind & Fire.................................Graham A. Fisher
It's Me, O Lord..Members of Heswall Churches
Companion to the Fylde..R.K. Davies
Country Walks on Merseyside...David Parry
A-Z Cheshire Ghosts..Muriel Armand

OTHER TITLES FROM WIRRAL LIBRARIES

Birkenhead of Yesteryear..Carol Bidston
Della Robbia Pottery, Birkenhead..David Hillhouse
Hooton to West Kirby Branch Line ....Merseyside Railway History Group
The People's Garden...Clifford Thornton
Up Our Lobby ....Bill Houldin
Wirral Visions ....Heather and Douglas Wilson